CAREC TOURISM STRATEGY 2030

DECEMBER 2020

CAREC
Central Asia Regional Economic Cooperation Program

ADB

Contents

Tables and Figures iv

Abbreviations v

Executive Summary vi

I.   Introduction 1

II. Global Tourism Trends and Impact of COVID-19 2

III. Tourism in the CAREC Region 5
    A.   Domestic, Inbound, and Outbound Tourism 5
    B.   Tourism Contribution to Gross Domestic Product and Competitiveness 8
    C.   CAREC Region's Potential for Attracting Core Tourism Segments 9
    D.   National Tourism Priorities and the Need for a Regional Tourism Strategy 13

IV. CAREC Tourism Strategy 2030 15
    A.   Vision 15
    B.   Guiding Principles 15
    C.   CAREC Tourism Development Concept and Regional Tourism Priority Clusters 16

V. Strategic Pillars of the CAREC Tourism Strategy 2030 19
    A.   Strategic Pillar 1: Connectivity and Infrastructure 21
    B.   Strategic Pillar 2: Quality and Standards 22
    C.   Strategic Pillar 3: Skills Development 23
    D.   Strategic Pillar 4: Marketing and Branding 24
    E.   Strategic Pillar 5: Market Intelligence 25
    F.   Cross-Cutting Themes 26

VI. Institutionalization and Implementation Arrangements 28
    A.   Phased Implementation Approach 28
    B.   Institutional Structure 29
    C.   Financing 31
    D.   Partnerships 31
    E.   Results Framework 32

Appendixes
    1.   Summary of CAREC Countries' Tourism Strategies 33
    2.   Indicative List of Provinces and Cities under Each Priority Tourism Cluster 37
    3.   Regional Tourism Investment Framework (2021–2025) 39
    4.   Results Framework 45

Tables and Figures

Tables

1 Main Motivations for Traveling to CAREC Countries, 2019 7
2 Strengths, Weaknesses, Opportunities, and Threats Analysis 20

A1 Summary of CAREC Countries' Tourism Strategies 33
A2 Indicative List of Provinces and Cities under Each Priority Tourism Cluster 37
A3.1 Strategic Pillar 1—Connectivity and Infrastructure 39
A3.2 Strategic Pillar 2—Quality and Standards 42
A3.3 Strategic Pillar 3—Skills Development 42
A3.4 Strategic Pillar 4—Marketing and Branding 43
A3.5 Strategic Pillar 5—Market Intelligence 44
A4 Results Framework 45

Figures

1 Distribution of Domestic Tourists in CAREC Countries, 2019 5
2 Inbound Tourists in CAREC Countries, 2019 6
3 Outbound Tourists from CAREC Countries, 2019 7
4 Travel and Tourism Competitiveness and Direct Contribution to Gross Domestic Product.... 9
5 CAREC Tourism Development Concept and Clusters 18
6 CAREC Tourism Strategic Pillars 21
7 CAREC Institutional Framework 30

Abbreviations

ADB	Asian Development Bank
CAGR	compound annual growth rate
CAREC	Central Asia Regional Economic Cooperation
COVID-19	coronavirus disease
GDP	gross domestic product
MICE	meetings, conventions, conferences, and exhibitions
PPP	public–private partnership
PRC	People's Republic of China
SMEs	small and medium-sized enterprises
UNESCO	United Nations Educational, Scientific and Cultural Organization
UNWTO	United Nations World Tourism Organization
WTTC	World Travel and Tourism Council

Executive Summary

The Central Asia Regional Economic Cooperation (CAREC) Tourism Strategy 2030 provides a common strategic and holistic framework to guide tourism operations in the CAREC region until 2030. It sets out the long-term vision, guiding principles, strategic pillars, and targets to promote sustainable, safe, and inclusive tourism development in the region and enhance the region's attraction as a competitive tourism destination globally. It builds on the findings and recommendations of *Promoting Regional Tourism Cooperation under CAREC 2030*, a scoping study published in 2019. The tourism strategy is aligned with the overall directions of the CAREC 2030 strategy as well as with CAREC countries' tourism priorities and plans, and it seeks to ensure close coordination among tourism initiatives being implemented by development partners in the region.

The coronavirus disease (COVID-19) outbreak in early 2020 has placed significant pressure on CAREC economies, with tourism being one of the most severely impacted sectors. International tourist arrivals decreased by 65% globally during January–June 2020 compared to the same period in 2019. According to estimates of the United Nations World Tourism Organization (UNWTO), the overall reduction in international tourist arrivals worldwide in 2020 could range from 58% to 78%, depending on when travel restrictions are lifted. As a result, the preference of travelers is shifting toward closer, safer, and uncrowded destinations, and countries are adapting their tourism strategies and plans to focus on domestic and intra-regional tourism in the short term. The CAREC Tourism Strategy 2030 takes into consideration the impacts and trends resulting from the COVID-19 pandemic. Through the gradual implementation of regional projects and initiatives across its five strategic pillars, it seeks to help CAREC countries' tourism sectors bounce back stronger and faster, and restore travelers' confidence and trust by promoting the region as a safe and resilient tourism destination.

The CAREC region possesses a wide range of historical and cultural heritage, unique gastronomy and local traditions, a rich and unexplored network of cities, and arresting natural endowments that traverse national boundaries. In 2019, the CAREC countries received 424 million domestic tourists and 41 reducing regional imbalances and million foreign tourists. Domestic tourists and visitors from neighboring countries travel mainly for business purposes and for visiting friends and relatives, particularly on short trips of 2–3 days. On the other hand, foreign tourists from distant countries tend to be motivated by culture and heritage, nature and adventure, and business. Thus, the CAREC Tourism Strategy 2030 aims at supporting the development of unique tourism products and experiences catering to various tourism segments such as business, culture, nature and adventure, sun and beach holidays, health and wellness, and domestic weekenders.

Vision, Guiding Principles, and Priority Tourism Clusters

The CAREC Tourism Strategy 2030 is inspired by a vision to create *"a sustainable, safe, easily accessible, and well-known tourism region that provides a variety of unique year-round quality experiences to visitors along the Silk Road, and widely shares its benefits among its communities."*

Five guiding principles underpin the development of comprehensive and effective regional tourism programs and the promotion of tourism cooperation in the region: (i) prioritizing quality over quantity to ensure environmental, social, and cultural sustainability; (ii) adapting to global trends and building resilience by promoting the uniqueness of countries' tourism products while building regional synergies and creating greater opportunities for economies of scale and optimization of resources to effectively respond to new global and regional developments; (iii) reducing regional imbalances and empowering local communities; (iv) promoting multi-seasonal tourism through product diversification and promotion of multicountry trips to help address seasonality and provide year-round opportunities for businesses in the region; and (v) adopting a holistic and phased approach for developing the CAREC tourism network along the Silk Road and ensuring sustainable development of the regional tourism clusters.

The Silk Road is the most important route linking CAREC countries' major cities and tourism assets. In addition, major national and transnational roads in the region are also connected to the Silk Road, such as the Pamir Highway, Karakorum Highway, Chinggis Khaan Trail, and Trans-Siberian Railway. The CAREC Tourism Strategy 2030 identifies seven priority regional tourism clusters connected to these main tourist routes. The priority tourism clusters have been selected based on their regional relevance; visitation levels; and future development potential to attract an increasing number of tourists, increase spending per tourist, and improve the contribution of the tourism sector to countries' gross domestic product (GDP).

The seven priority cluster groups are as follows: (i) Caspian, covering Azerbaijan, Georgia, Kazakhstan, and Turkmenistan; (ii) Heart of Central Asia, covering Afghanistan, Kazakhstan, the Kyrgyz Republic, Tajikistan, Turkmenistan, and Uzbekistan; (iii) Almaty–Bishkek, referring to the area of the Almaty–Bishkek Economic Corridor and the Tian Shan mountains, covering Kazakhstan, the Kyrgyz Republic, and north Xinjiang Uyghur Autonomous Region in the People's Republic of China (PRC); (iv) Golden Coast, located in the southwest of Pakistan; (v) Karakorum–Wakhan, covering the eastern part of Afghanistan, north Pakistan, northwest Xinjiang Uyghur Autonomous Region, and southeast Tajikistan; (vi) Altai, covering Kazakhstan, Mongolia, and the PRC; and (vii) Gobi and Grasslands, covering Inner Mongolia Autonomous Region in the PRC and Mongolia.

Strategic Pillars

While CAREC countries possess outstanding natural and cultural resources, there are still several factors that hinder the development of their tourism sectors. These include limited access to and between CAREC countries, complex and nonuniform visa requirements and border arrangements, inconsistent quality of tourism infrastructure and services, skills shortages, lack of reliable tourism data and statistics, and low awareness and knowledge about the tourist attractions in CAREC countries. To achieve its long-term vision and overcome these challenges through enhanced cooperation, the CAREC Tourism Strategy 2030 identifies five strategic pillars:

(i) **Connectivity and infrastructure.** This includes the improvement of air and land connectivity; simplification of border crossing procedures; harmonization of visa requirements; and improvement of tourism infrastructure facilities, and urban development in areas with potential for year-round activities within the priority tourism clusters.

(ii) **Quality and standards.** This includes the development and implementation of effective and harmonized minimum quality, hygiene, and environmental standards. This could include the development of a "Silk Road Quality Label" for tourism services, to be adopted on a voluntary basis.

(iii) **Skills development.** This focuses on addressing the gaps between industry practices and tourism education and training provision, and developing integrated regional trainings and programs for both public and private tourism stakeholders, maximizing the use of digital technologies.

(iv) **Marketing and branding.** This includes building the common brand ("Visit Silk Road") through development and operationalization of the CAREC tourism web portal, and organization of joint tourism promotion activities and events and business-to-business initiatives for tour operators and other tourism services business providers.

(v) **Market intelligence.** This includes development and implementation of common methodologies for data gathering and production of tourism statistics following international best practices, and promotion of partnerships between public and private tourism stakeholders in the region for conducting joint market research to better understand customers' preferences, desired experiences, and needs.

In addition, the following themes cut across all the strategic pillars: (i) health, safety, and security to support countries' efforts in responding to the COVID-19 pandemic and to build resilience of their tourism sectors to future global crises; (ii) digital and communication technologies; (iii) gender equality; (iv) private sector development; (v) environmental sustainability through the adoption of sustainability practices to protect the region's tourism assets; and (vi) universal access to integrate the needs of differently abled people and elderly travelers into destination planning and management.

Implementation and Institutional Arrangements

A phased approach will be adopted for the implementation of the CAREC Tourism Strategy 2030 and in the prioritization of initiatives and projects under the strategic pillars. During the initial phase, from 2021 to 2023, regional interventions will focus on domestic and intra-regional tourism. The second phase, from 2024 to 2028, will focus on attracting high-spending international markets through improvement of air connectivity and development of joint tourism products and multicountry experiences. In the last phase, from 2029 onward, expansion toward secondary destinations beyond the seven priority regional tourism clusters will be considered. To support this, a regional tourism investment framework has been developed, covering regional projects and initiatives under the five strategic pillars to be implemented during the first 5 years of the strategy implementation period (2021–2025).

The CAREC tourism work will be led and coordinated by a CAREC tourism focal points group. An incremental approach is envisioned to effectively build the countries' ownership and devise the most appropriate institutional structure based on progress made over time. As a first step, focused and demand-driven technical expert groups will be formed either at the thematic or cluster level to further develop regional projects and initiatives within the strategic pillars. When progress is considered sufficient and based on countries' demand, a small centralized tourism office and/or an independent regional tourism agency with common funding mechanisms could be established.

The CAREC tourism focal points group will be responsible for monitoring the implementation of the tourism strategy and the regional investment framework. Recognizing the global, changing nature of the sector and the fact that progress may be different within the strategic pillars and/or tourism clusters, adjustments will be made as needed based on countries' emerging needs and priorities.

Given the cross-cutting nature of the tourism sector, careful consideration will be given to establish an effective mechanism for coordination among the wide range of stakeholders, including government agencies, the private sector, academia, and civil society. Technical, analytical, and organizational support will be provided by the CAREC Secretariat, development partners, and the CAREC Institute. Efforts will be devoted to mobilizing greater financing from a wide range of sources, including from development partners, state budgets, the private sector, and public–private partnership (PPP) arrangements. In addition, the establishment of a regional investment fund to support tourism investments with a regional scope and impact will be explored.

CHAPTER I

Introduction

1. The Central Asia Regional Economic Cooperation (CAREC) Program is a partnership of 11 countries and development partners working together to promote development through cooperation, leading to accelerated economic growth and shared prosperity. CAREC operations are guided by the CAREC 2030 strategy endorsed at the 16th CAREC Ministerial Conference in October 2017.[1] The CAREC 2030 strategy focuses on five operational clusters, including the trade, tourism, and economic corridors development cluster.

2. Tourism transcends national borders, and there are a range of benefits for countries within a geographic region working with each other in the development, management, and promotion of their tourism sectors. Regional tourism cooperation can help strengthen economic, social, and cultural ties among countries, thereby enhancing the region's image and making it more attractive for foreign visitors and investment. Developing a regional approach also creates a larger market for supply and demand of tourism services, and offers greater diversity and a wider range of experiences for travelers and tourists. The overall goal of such cooperation is to improve living standards for the populations of CAREC countries and accelerate inclusive economic growth in the region.

3. In 2018, the CAREC Secretariat undertook a scoping study on Promoting Regional Tourism Cooperation under CAREC 2030 to assess the potential of CAREC as a regional cooperation platform to promote a coordinated approach to tourism development.[2] The study identified opportunities for enhancing and expanding tourism cooperation among CAREC member countries and maximizing economic opportunities while safeguarding ecosystems.

4. Building on the findings of the scoping study, the CAREC Tourism Strategy 2030 sets out the long-term vision, objectives, programs, and targets to promote sustainable, safe, and inclusive tourism development in the region and to enhance the region's attraction as a competitive tourism destination globally. It builds upon countries' efforts in this area as well as initiatives being implemented by development partners. It adopts a holistic approach, covering travel facilitation and connectivity, human resources and skills development, tourism infrastructure and services, digitalization, tourism marketing and promotion, and regional institutional arrangements for tourism, including the roles of both the public and private sectors.

---

[1]   Asian Development Bank (ADB). 2017. *CAREC 2030: Connecting the Region for Shared and Sustainable Development*. Manila.
[2]   ADB. 2019. *Promoting Regional Tourism Cooperation under CAREC 2030: A Scoping Study*. Manila.

CHAPTER II

Global Tourism Trends and Impact of COVID-19

5. The global tourism industry has been growing robustly over the past 2 decades, showing strong resilience through several crisis periods. Since 2000, international tourism growth, with a compound annual growth rate (CAGR) of 5.8%, has outpaced the growth of the global economy (5.4% CAGR).[3] As of 2018, the tourism industry directly contributed 3.9% ($3.35 trillion) to the world's gross domestic product (GDP), of which 71% corresponded to domestic tourism and 29% to inbound tourism expenditure.[4] Its value added stood at 58.8% of the revenues ($5.7 trillion).[5]

6. The growth of the tourism industry globally has been driven mainly by the increasing middle class from emerging economies. Moreover, countries in Asia and South America have experienced robust growth in per capita income, which has enabled consumers in these regions to take more overseas trips.

7. The global spread of the coronavirus disease (COVID-19) outbreak in early 2020 has severely impacted the tourism sector. From January to June 2020, global international tourist arrivals decreased by 65%, with Asia and the Pacific experiencing an especially hard decline in tourist arrivals of 72%. According to estimates of the United Nations World Tourism Organization (UNWTO), the overall reduction in international tourist arrivals worldwide in 2020 could range from 58% to 78%, depending on when travel restrictions are lifted. This could result in a loss of export revenues from tourism in the range of $910 million–$1.2 trillion and could put at risk up to 120 million jobs in the tourism industry.[6] While domestic tourism is expected to recover more quickly, prospects are that regional and international travel will not show any signs of recovery until 2021.

8. The global COVID-19 pandemic is expected to create new patterns and trends in the tourism sector, particularly in the short term. These include the following:

(i) **Increased importance of domestic and regional tourism.** The COVID-19 outbreak will shift travelers' priorities to closer, safer, and uncrowded destinations. Thus, domestic and regional tourism could be the more sought-after alternative, with the car being the preferred mode of transport to avoid contact with large groups of people. Villas or accommodation units with self-catering facilities compliant with social distancing requirements will experience the highest demand during the recovery period. This trend also means a

---

[3]   United Nations World Tourism Organization (UNWTO). 2020. *World Tourism Barometer*. 18(1). Madrid; World Bank. World Bank Open Data (accessed 10 August 2020).

[4]   World Travel and Tourism Council (WTTC). 2019. *Travel and Tourism Economic Impact*. London. The data are from 2018. This refers to domestic tourism expenditure (i.e., tourism expenditure of a resident visitor within the economy of reference) and inbound tourism expenditure (i.e., tourism expenditure of a non-resident visitor within the economy of reference). UNWTO. Glossary of Tourism Terms (accessed 30 October 2020).

[5]   WTTC. 2019. *Travel and Tourism Economic Impact*. London.

[6]   UNWTO. 2020. *World Tourism Barometer*. 18(5). Madrid.

more regionalized pattern of business travel. Long-haul air travel will potentially resume at a fast pace only once the contamination risks disappear and when a COVID-19 vaccine is put into use.

(ii) **Emergence of safe travel corridors.** Although COVID-19 cases are continuing to rise, some countries have been successful in containing the pandemic through the adoption of several public health and social measures. Such measures, however, have negatively affected economic growth. In an attempt to revamp the economy and reactivate the tourism industry, countries are reestablishing connections and partnering to develop virus-free travel bubbles, which offer a safe environment for the development of tourist activities, protecting both tourists and the local population.[7]

9. In addition, the following trends are also foreseen to influence the tourism sector globally in the coming years:

(i) **Greater focus on sustainability and responsible travel.** An increasing share of tourists are paying more attention to the environmental footprint and the socioeconomic impact of their travels. Tourists increasingly prefer destinations and businesses with clear sustainability policies, recycling procedures, and other circular economy solutions, and there is a growing interest in tourism products and experiences that can help protect the environment and bring tangible benefits to local communities.[8]

(ii) **Technological innovations.** The process of digitalization of the tourism sector is changing the business model of suppliers and the expectations of customers. The emergence of new players in accommodation (e.g., Airbnb, HomeAway), transport (BlaBlaCar, Uber), catering (Eatwith), and guiding (ToursByLocals) services has revolutionized the tourism sector. "Smart tourism destinations"[9] are comprehensively managing tourist visits, augmented reality solutions are improving the experience of customers, virtual reality is increasingly being applied to meetings and conferences, cryptocurrencies are starting to be used to pay for services, 5G connections and Wi-Fi are becoming necessary services, and the Internet of Things and artificial intelligence are already being applied by many hotel chains and other tourism services providers.

(iii) **Customers as the main source of information through online platforms.** Word-of-mouth has been always an important factor when tourists select their travel destinations. Most travelers now fully rely on online platforms for planning and booking their trips. The increased use of social media and travel blogging has accentuated this trend, reducing the influence of mainstream traditional communication channels in destination choice. This represents a cost-effective marketing opportunity for lesser-known destinations to build a strong tourism brand and image perception among consumers in target markets and segments globally.

---

[7] Virus-free travel bubbles refer to partnerships among countries that have been successful in containing the pandemic and agree to open up borders and reestablish connections among them to allow entry of virus-free travelers and reactivate the tourism industry and related economic activity.

[8] According to the UNWTO, sustainable tourism refers to "tourism that takes full account of its current and future economic, social and environmental impacts, addressing the needs of visitors, the industry, the environment and host communities."

[9] E. Çeltek. 2020. *Handbook of Research on Smart Technology Applications in the Tourism Industry*. Hershey, Pennsylvania: IGI Global.; M. Castells. 2009. *The Rise of the Network Society,* 2nd edition. New Jersey: John Wiley & Sons, Ltd. A smart tourism destination is one that responds to the requirements of global mobile elites (increased mobility leads to the surge of a new social order in which a global well-connected leader-elite rules over a mass of disconnected people) by facilitating access to tourism and hospitality products, services, spaces, and experiences through information and communication technology-based tools. It also promotes innovative and entrepreneurial businesses and fosters interconnectedness of businesses.

(iv) **Experiential travel.** The traditional travel motivation of spending time away from home to relax is declining. Instead, tourists look for authentic experiences, learn while traveling, and spend a memorable time in the destination by interacting with local people and immersing themselves in the local culture, history, gastronomy, and traditions.[10] Destination management organizations, tour operators, and businesses need to adapt accordingly by developing and planning a set of unique and diversified experiences and providing personalized services. Increasing engagement with local communities is key for this purpose.

(v) **Further increase of middle-income class population and growing influence of younger generations.** The global middle-income class population is expected to reach 4.9 billion by 2033, with most of the growth occurring in the People's Republic of China (PRC).[11] This is expected to have a positive impact on the tourism sector given the high travel propensity and increased disposable income of this population group. Furthermore, tech-savvy and technology-driven age groups—such as millennials (also known as Gen Y) and Gen Z—have specific needs for communication, consumption, and tourism experiences.[12] These age groups are expected to represent 50% of all travelers by 2028.[13]

---

[10]   Experiential travel aims at getting a deeper understanding of a travel destination by closely connecting with its culture, people, and history. The traveler usually blends with locals (e.g., a friend, an accommodation host) who give guidance on how best to experience a place. Experiential travel tends to focus on travel that is inspirational, personalized, and/or creates a path to self-discovery.

[11]   H. Kharas. 2010. The Emerging Middle Class in Developing Countries. *Organisation for Economic Co-operation and Development, Development Centre Working Papers.* No. 285. Paris: Organisation for Economic Co-operation and Development.

[12]   Gen X defines the generation that was born during 1965–1980. Millennials (or Gen Y) were born during 1981–1996. Gen Z corresponds to people born during 1995–2015.

[13]   Horwath HTL. 2015. *Tourism Megatrends: 10 Things You Need to Know About the Future of Tourism.* New York.

CHAPTER III

Tourism in the CAREC Region

A. Domestic, Inbound, and Outbound Tourism[14]

10. Tourism in the CAREC region is mainly driven by domestic tourism, followed by tourists from neighboring countries, and lastly by tourists from geographically distant markets.[15] In 2019, the region received 424 million domestic tourists, highly concentrated in Uzbekistan (29.9%) and two regions in the PRC: Inner Mongolia Autonomous Region and Xinjiang Uyghur Autonomous Region (53.4%) (Figure 1).

Figure 1: Distribution of Domestic Tourists in CAREC Countries, 2019 (%)

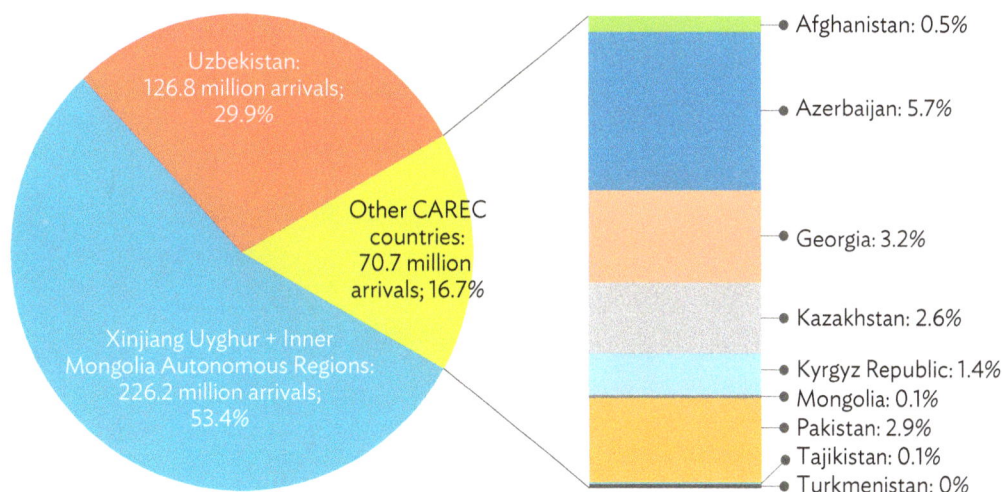

- Uzbekistan: 126.8 million arrivals; 29.9%
- Xinjiang Uyghur + Inner Mongolia Autonomous Regions: 226.2 million arrivals; 53.4%
- Other CAREC countries: 70.7 million arrivals; 16.7%

- Afghanistan: 0.5%
- Azerbaijan: 5.7%
- Georgia: 3.2%
- Kazakhstan: 2.6%
- Kyrgyz Republic: 1.4%
- Mongolia: 0.1%
- Pakistan: 2.9%
- Tajikistan: 0.1%
- Turkmenistan: 0%

CAREC = Central Asia Regional Economic Cooperation.
Sources: Estimates from the consultant team under Asian Development Bank. 2019. *Technical Assistance for Sustainable Tourism Development in the Central Asia Regional Economic Cooperation Region*. Manila. based on 2019 information provided by the Bureau of Statistics of the Xinjiang Uyghur Autonomous Region; Ministry of Environment and Tourism of Mongolia; Statistical Bulletin of the Inner Mongolia Autonomous Region; the United Nations World Tourism Organization. UNWTO Statistics Database (accessed 20 June 2020); and World Bank. 2020. *Global Economic Prospects*. Washington, DC.

[14] Domestic tourism comprises tourism-related activities of residents within their country of reference, inbound tourism comprises tourism-related activities in a country by visitors who are not residents of that country, and outbound tourism comprises tourism-related activities by residents outside their country of reference. A country sends outbound visitors and receives inbound visitors. Inbound visitors (arrivals) include both overnight tourists and same-day visitors (excursionists). United Nations, Department of Economic and Social Affairs, Statistics Division; and UNWTO. 2010. *International Recommendations for Tourism Statistics 2008*. New York.
[15] Neighboring countries refer to those that are within a 3-hour flight time from each CAREC country. This includes other CAREC countries if they meet the 3-hour flight time criterion.

11. In 2019, the region sent 70 million outbound tourists and received 41 million tourists. International tourism in the region (both inbound and outbound) is highly concentrated in neighboring countries, particularly in the Russian Federation. More than three-quarters of the total foreign arrivals are concentrated in four countries: Kazakhstan (23.6%), the Kyrgyz Republic (20.2%), Georgia (18.6%), and Uzbekistan (16.3%). Of the total inbound tourists, 91% come from neighboring countries, of which two-thirds of the total arrive from other CAREC countries (Figure 2).

12. Although outbound tourism is less concentrated than inbound tourism, tourists from four CAREC countries represent two-thirds of the total: the PRC (23.3%),[16] Uzbekistan (17.9%), Kazakhstan (15.6%), and Azerbaijan (10.2%). Of the total outbound tourists, 83% travel to neighboring countries, although only half of them go to other CAREC countries (Figure 3). There are, however, some notable differences across countries. For instance, almost all outbound tourists from Uzbekistan travel to other CAREC countries while, in the case of Pakistan, only 4.5% travel within the CAREC region. Other main destinations for outbound tourists include Iran, the Republic of Korea, the Russian Federation, and Turkey.

13. Travel motivations in the CAREC countries (Table 1) vary substantially between domestic tourists, tourists from neighboring countries, and tourists from distant countries. Domestic

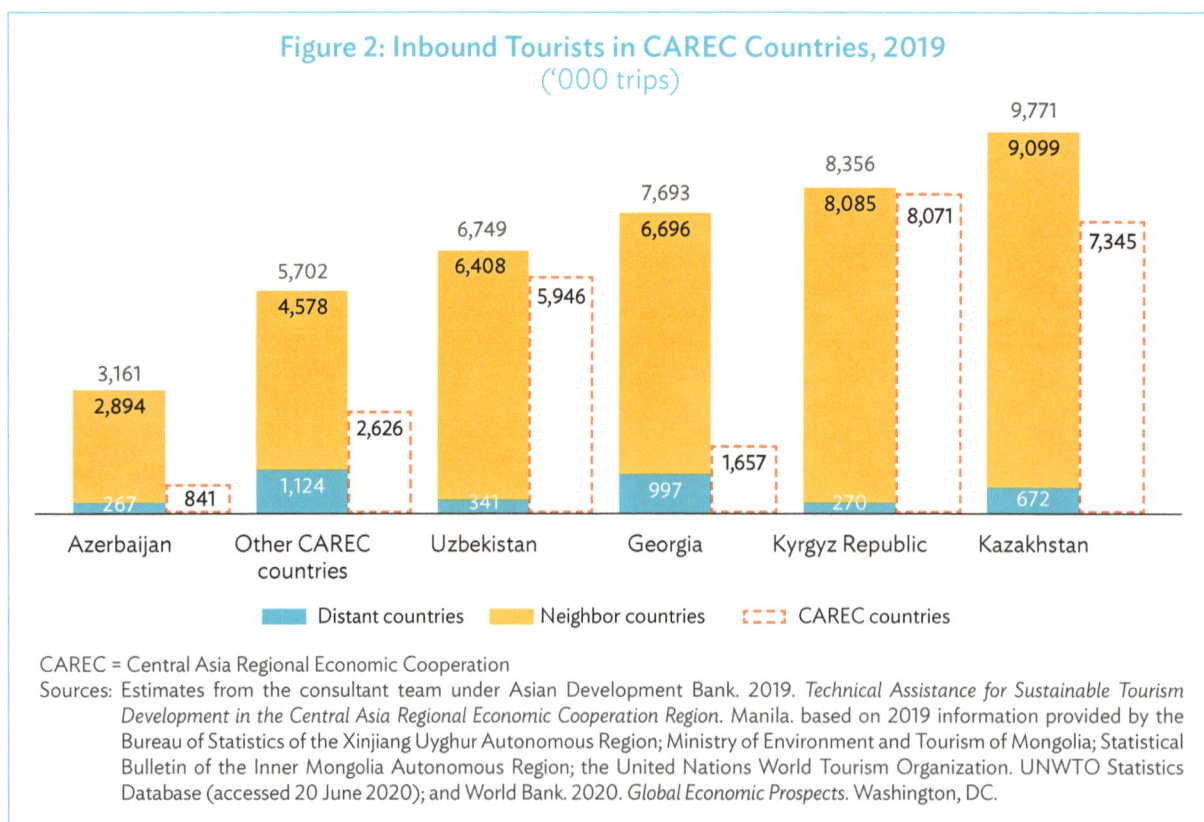

Figure 2: Inbound Tourists in CAREC Countries, 2019
('000 trips)

CAREC = Central Asia Regional Economic Cooperation
Sources: Estimates from the consultant team under Asian Development Bank. 2019. *Technical Assistance for Sustainable Tourism Development in the Central Asia Regional Economic Cooperation Region*. Manila. based on 2019 information provided by the Bureau of Statistics of the Xinjiang Uyghur Autonomous Region; Ministry of Environment and Tourism of Mongolia; Statistical Bulletin of the Inner Mongolia Autonomous Region; the United Nations World Tourism Organization. UNWTO Statistics Database (accessed 20 June 2020); and World Bank. 2020. *Global Economic Prospects*. Washington, DC.

---

[16]   This refers only to the two PRC regions that are part of the CAREC Program: the Inner Mongolia Autonomous Region and the Xinjiang Uyghur Autonomous Region.

tourists and tourists from neighboring countries travel mainly for business purposes and for visiting friends and relatives, while tourists from distant countries tend to be motivated by culture and heritage, nature and adventure, and business.

Figure 3: Outbound Tourists from CAREC Countries, 2019
('000 trips)

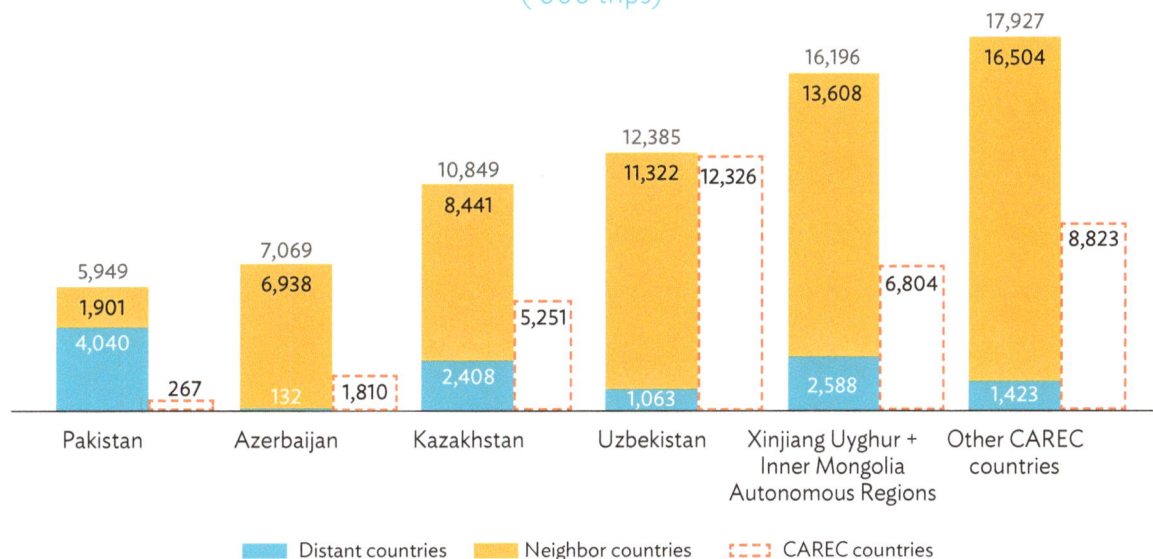

CAREC = Central Asia Regional Economic Cooperation
Sources: Estimates from the consultant team under Asian Development Bank. 2019. *Technical Assistance for Sustainable Tourism Development in the Central Asia Regional Economic Cooperation Region*. Manila. based on 2019 information provided by the Bureau of Statistics of the Xinjiang Uyghur Autonomous Region; Ministry of Environment and Tourism of Mongolia; Statistical Bulletin of the Inner Mongolia Autonomous Region; the United Nations World Tourism Organization. UNWTO Statistics Database (accessed 20 June 2020); and World Bank. 2020. *Global Economic Prospects*. Washington, DC.

Table 1: Main Motivations for Traveling to CAREC Countries, 2019
(%)

Market Segment	Inbound Tourists		
	Domestic	Neighboring Countries	Distant Markets
Business and MICE	20.94	23.52	16.63
Visiting friends and relatives	20.01	20.85	7.40
Nature, sports, and adventure	13.10	16.17	26.95
Culture and heritage	13.63	15.82	32.80
Holiday, sun, and beach	17.01	14.88	7.91
City breaks	15.31	8.76	8.31

MICE = meetings, incentives, conferences, and exhibitions.
Source: Tour operator's survey under Asian Development Bank. 2019. *Technical Assistance for Sustainable Tourism Development in the Central Asia Regional Economic Cooperation Region*. Manila.

B. Tourism Contribution to Gross Domestic Product and Competitiveness

14. Tourism impact on GDP is a function of the quantity of tourists, their spending, and the value added generated by that spending.[17] Figure 4 shows the international competitive positioning of CAREC countries. The vertical axis represents the score of the Travel and Tourism Competitiveness Index from the World Economic Forum (with a global average of 3.87). The average score of CAREC countries is 3.66, ranging from 3.10 in Pakistan to 4.88 in the PRC.[18] The horizontal axis corresponds to the direct contribution of the tourism sector to the GDP in each country (with a global average of 4.3%). Internationally, compared to similar economies,[19] CAREC countries' tourism sectors tend to have lower direct contributions to their respective GDPs, ranging from as high as 9.4% in Georgia to as low as 0.1% in Turkmenistan.[20] In terms of appropriation of revenues from the tourism sector, there are also notable differences, including high appropriation in Pakistan (63.7%),[21] medium appropriation in Azerbaijan (36.9%) and Uzbekistan (54.1%), and low appropriation in the two PRC regions (about 20%) and the Kyrgyz Republic (15.7%).

15. Countries can increase tourism's direct impact on GDP through two distinct strategies: (i) a volume-based strategy (i.e., mass tourism with little spending and appropriation of value added), or (ii) a high-value strategy (i.e., low tourism volume but high spending and appropriation of value added). Although the GDP effects derived from both strategies could be the same, the social and environmental sustainability impacts are quite different, as more tourists tend to produce higher social and environmental negative externalities. Well-designed tourism strategies, therefore, strike a good balance between volume of tourists, spending per tourist, appropriation of value added, and sustainability from a social and environmental perspective.

16. Tourism is considered a priority sector in CAREC countries' strategies and plans. However, the level of global competitiveness of their tourism sectors is quite low.[22] Although CAREC countries have abundant and attractive natural and cultural assets, they have shortcomings in other critical dimensions such as transport and tourism services infrastructure. Tackling these dimensions is, therefore, key to improving overall visitation and spending levels. Strengthening the tourism value chain by improving the range and quality of tourism services and increasing the

---

[17] This refers to what part of every dollar spent by tourists (domestic and foreign) in the country contributes directly to the GDP through national value added. Countries with high percentages of national value added in the spending levels have a greater appropriation of value in the value chain than countries that have low levels of value added from tourism revenues.

[18] Travel and Tourism Competitiveness Index scores are not available for Afghanistan, Turkmenistan, and Uzbekistan.

[19] Examples are Cambodia, Côte D'Ivoire, Guatemala, the Philippines, Rwanda, and Senegal. The primary reason for the choice of such countries is the size of their economies, the level of development of the tourism industry, and the tourism products offered.

[20] World Economic Forum. 2019. *The Travel & Tourism Competitiveness Report 2019: Travel and Tourism at a Tipping Point*. Geneva; WTTC. 2019. *Travel and Tourism Economic Impact*. London; and World Bank. World Bank Open Data (accessed 10 August 2020). For Afghanistan and Turkmenistan, data have been estimated by the consultant team under ADB. 2019. *Technical Assistance for Sustainable Tourism Development in the Central Asia Regional Economic Cooperation Region*. Manila.

[21] The appropriation is measured as a ratio between direct contribution of tourism to GDP (numerator) and tourism revenues (denominator). The world average is 58.8%.

[22] The World Economic Forum's Travel and Tourism Competitiveness Index is used to measure the international competitiveness of the tourism sector of a country, and can be used as (i) an indicator of the effectiveness of countries' planning processes, (ii) a guide on which key issues and areas need to be tackled, and (iii) a means of prioritizing the utilization of scarce resources to maximize benefits. The PRC as a whole is highly competitive internationally. However, the two CAREC regions (the Inner Mongolia Autonomous Region and the Xinjiang Uyghur Autonomous Region) lag behind the national results and therefore are more in line with the other CAREC countries.

Figure 4: Travel and Tourism Competitiveness and Direct Contribution to Gross Domestic Product

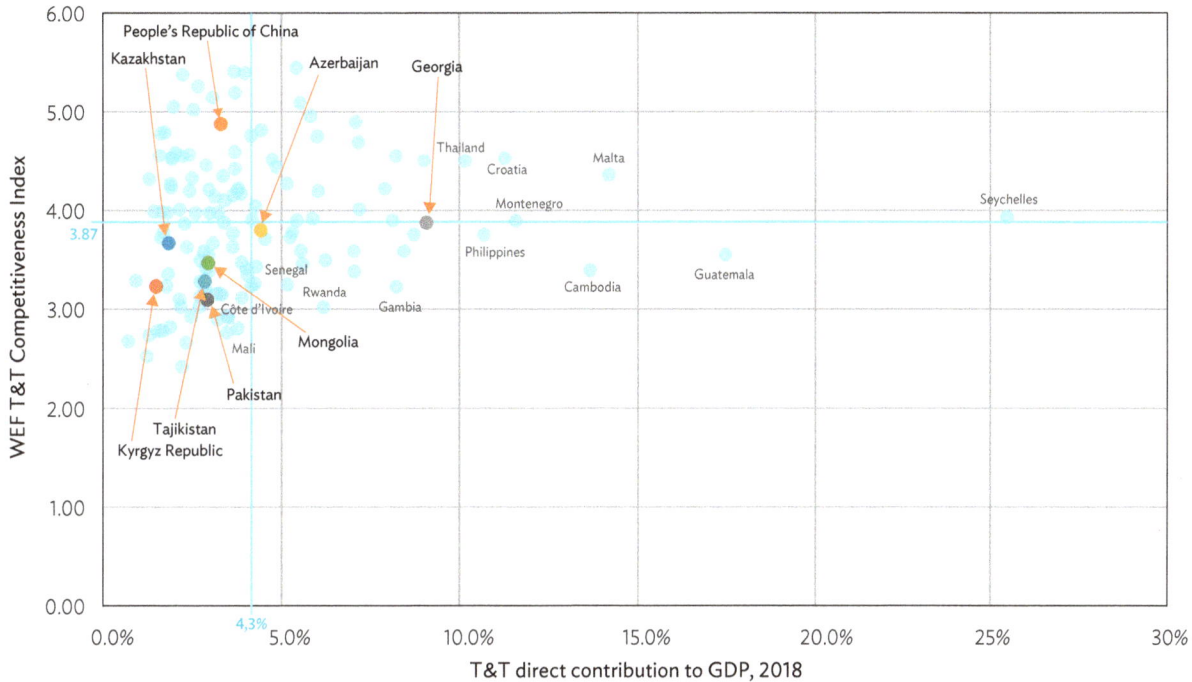

GDP = gross domestic product, T&T = travel and tourism, WEF = World Economic Forum.

Sources: WEF. 2019. *The Travel & Tourism Competitiveness Report 2019: Travel and Tourism at a Tipping Point*. Geneva; World Travel and Tourism Council (WTTC). 2019. *Travel and Tourism Economic Impact*. London; and World Bank. World Bank Open Data (accessed 10 August 2020).

participation of local small and medium-sized enterprises (SMEs) and other private sector stakeholders will allow CAREC countries to improve the national appropriation of tourism revenues.

C. CAREC Region's Potential for Attracting Core Tourism Segments

17. CAREC is a heterogeneous region with areas and routes rich in history and culture and arresting natural endowments that traverse national boundaries. The capitals and important metropolitan areas in the region constitute a rich and unexplored network of cities capable of providing unique experiences catering to various tourism segments such as business, culture, nature and adventure, sun and beach holidays, and health and wellness, among others. In addition, domestic weekenders are critical for sustainable tourism development, particularly considering the challenges faced by the tourism industry because of the COVID-19 outbreak. Domestic weekenders can help flatten the seasonality curve, generating year-round business to regional tourism sites and the SMEs associated with those sites, while being the driving force of domestic tourism in a region where the majority of the population lives in urban areas. Thus, CAREC countries can also cater for this market segment through the offer of 2- to 3-day trips around the major cities,

with activities that engage families or groups in different activities (e.g., adventure, religion, culture, nature, shopping, etc.).

18. **Business and meetings, incentives, conferences, and exhibitions tourism.** Internationally, city and business trips account for 27.6% of the total global outbound trips.[23] The CAREC region is strategically located between some of the largest economic regions of the world such as Europe, northeast Asia, and the Middle East. Several capitals or major cities (Almaty, Baku, Bishkek, Hohhot, Islamabad, Karachi, Tashkent, Tbilisi, and Urumqi) in the CAREC region offer the unique potential of year-round city-break and business-related opportunities.[24] Other cities offer good part-of-year potential, such as Batumi, Cholpon-Ata, Kashgar, Lahore, and Nur-Sultan. However, less than 1% of global meetings take place in the CAREC region.[25] This is mostly because of the limited air connectivity between CAREC countries and international markets as well as the complex visa regimes and entry requirements in the region. Less than half of all country pairs within the CAREC region are served with direct flights, and flight frequencies are generally low.[26]

19. Business customers look for personalized service, safe and comfortable transport, attractive urban design and well-functioning cities, clean and comfortable accommodation, good catering, and meeting venues. With the development of communication technologies, business events are becoming hybrid, combining the traditional aspect of physical presence of participants with remote contributions and online presentations. Thus, state-of-the-art technology and high-speed internet capability are a must. CAREC countries need to further improve the quality of these tourism-related services to further unleash the potential of meetings, incentives, conferences, and exhibitions (MICE) tourism in the region.

20. Small- and/or medium-scale meetings and conventions could be the core sector in which CAREC countries compete, since it would be complicated to divert large-scale events from the major capitals of Europe, East Asia, and North America. Events in CAREC countries should be as unique and localized as possible, engaging business travelers intellectually and emotionally, and linking the objective of the event with the local community, cultural traditions, and gastronomy.[27] The attractiveness of lesser-known and minor cities in CAREC countries could be improved by providing discounts or offering promotional rates to attract MICE buyers and improving the urban infrastructure and services such as 24/7 electricity, water supply and sanitation, transport, and connectivity. In terms of promotion and business development activity, CAREC countries could target MICE intermediaries and attend specialized MICE trade shows.[28]

---

[23]   UNWTO. 2020. *World Tourism Barometer.* 18(1). Madrid; and ITB Berlin. 2018. *ITB Berlin and IPK International: International City Trips—A Success Story.* Berlin.

[24]   These cities have the unique feature of allowing multi-seasonal city-related tourism with the attractiveness of their respective outskirts, which could result in higher occupancy rates for hotels and resorts. Other major cities in the region are only suitable for city tourism, stopovers, or activities complementary to business trips in 9 months of the year.

[25]   International Congress and Convention Association (ICCA). 2018. *The International Association Meetings Market 2018.* Amsterdam.

[26]   ADB. 2018. *Aviation and the Role of CAREC: A Scoping Study.* Manila.

[27]   Examples of related activities include traveling the Silk Road, going on a caravanning adventure, staying in a yurt, experiencing local horse culture, and tasting unique local foods.

[28]   These intermediaries include the European Federation of Associations of Professional Congress Organizers, International Association of Professional Congress Organizers, International Congress and Convention Association, Joint Meetings Industry Council, and Society of Incentive and Travel Executives.

21. **Nature and adventure.** In 2016, the adventure market was worth $445 million globally and was growing by 17.6% annually.[29] "Soft adventure," the largest segment, is expected to represent 62.4% of the total market by 2023.[30] Despite the COVID-19 situation, adventure tourists have a resilient motivation, are less sensitive than other segments to sanitary issues, and typically travel to remote areas. Hence, adventure tourism demand is likely to recover faster than other segments. Adventure travelers increasingly seek a personal connection with locals, interacting amicably around shared experiences. Among adventure tourists, solo travelers are a relatively small group, but they represent an important target for operators, as their spending tends to be higher, as well as the related margins.

22. The variety and multiplicity of natural endowments across the CAREC region offer the potential for year-round nature-based and ecotourism (adventure, sports, and ecology) in the region's mountain ranges, coastal areas, deserts, lakes, rivers, natural parks, and protected areas. The development of nature-based tourism in the region should include community-based tourism initiatives that allow visitors to interact with locals and provide an authentic and unique travel experience (e.g., skills development programs for communities on the preservation of tourism assets, tour guiding and walking tours, foreign languages, homestays).

23. In addition, the region has a unique ski and winter tourism potential, which could be combined with city trips around main air hubs (e.g., Almaty, Baku, Bishkek, Islamabad, Tashkent) and other unique areas such as northern Afghanistan, Altai, Georgia, Karakol, Karakorum, Khyber Pakhtunkhwa, Pamir, and Wakhan Corridor. Ski tourists mostly come from domestic markets, complemented by tourists from neighboring countries. CAREC countries should focus on fostering a ski culture among domestic travelers, while seeking to attract customers from neighboring countries and markets with high national ski participation rates (e.g., Czech Republic, Latvia, Poland, Slovakia). Investments in specialized state-of-the-art infrastructure with harmonized service standards and complementary services will be required for this purpose.

24. **Culture and heritage.** The Silk Road is the most important tourism asset linking countries in the CAREC region. It is the world's longest cultural route network connecting Asia and Europe with hundreds of historic buildings and monuments, caravansaries, ports, and cities, linking religions, cultures, ideas, knowledge, trade, and businesses. In 2018, 170 million international tourists identified culture as their main travel motivation (14.0% of total international arrivals), and 396 million (32.8%) considered cultural activities as part of their trip.[31]

---

[29]   Adventure Travel Trade Association. 2018. *Adventure Tourism Development Index*. Monroe, Washington.
[30]   "Soft adventure" refers to low-risk activities requiring little experience or skills, such as bird-watching, fishing, hunting, and joining a research expedition or safari. On the other hand, "hard adventure" refers to high-risk activities requiring higher skill levels, such as caving, climbing, hiking, horseback riding, kayaking, sailing, scuba diving, snorkeling, skiing and snowboarding, surfing, and trekking.
[31]   UNWTO. 2018. *Tourism and Culture Synergies*. Madrid.

25. The cultural heritage of the CAREC countries reflects the legacy of the Silk Road and other relevant historical elements and figures (e.g., Alexander the Great, Indo-Islamic and Mughal architecture, Buddhist heritage,[32] ancient Christian heritage in Georgia, and Karakol as a multireligious center in the Kyrgyz Republic). All this rich heritage provides unique opportunities for potential historical and cultural tourism circuits linking various CAREC countries. Moreover, the CAREC region is deeply embedded in Islamic culture. In 2019, the Islamic tourism market was estimated to be worth $175 billion (excluding the Hajj and Umrah), of which Central Asia has a small share of only 7%, mostly concentrated in Azerbaijan and Uzbekistan.[33] This market has been growing at an average annual rate of 8.3% since 2016 and is expected to outpace the global tourism sector growth rate by 2030 (footnote 33).

26. The cultural links among CAREC countries should be further promoted to reinforce the region's cultural image and stimulate visits across various countries. Intangible cultural aspects such as local lifestyles and traditions should be put into value, with the aim of creating authentic experiences of tourist–resident interactions (e.g., cooking courses, yurt and nomadic living). Local tour operators and travel agencies are key for the development of this tourism segment, especially in CAREC countries, where many tourism attractions are difficult to reach, connections with the local population

may be difficult to form, and the standards of various accommodation structures are low (making it crucial to manage the expectations of visitors). As in the adventure and nature market segment, community-based tourism initiatives (such as improving local communities' skills in tour guiding and preservation of assets) will be crucial for enhancing the experiences of tourists, increasing their satisfaction, and ultimately encouraging their spending.

27. **Sun and beach.** Holiday, leisure, and recreation is by far the largest tourism market segment in the world, accounting for 818 million international outbound trips, or 56% of total global international trips in 2019.[34] This market is highly competitive and price sensitive. Destinations and facilities in this segment need to be able to constantly innovate their products to avoid losing their clientele and achieve strategic positioning and differentiation. The demand in this segment is mature, requires quality, and has a relatively high elasticity both to price and time to reach destination. Increased competition, associated with the boom in new intermediation business models, has generally reduced profit margins in the value chain of sun and beach tourism.[35]

28. In the CAREC region, the Black Sea coast of Georgia, the Caspian Sea, Issyk-Kul lake, and the south Pakistan coast are the most relevant tourism assets for this segment. Sun and beach customers are more risk averse than other types

---

[32]   Buddhism is prevalent in Afghanistan, Kazakhstan, the Kyrgyz Republic, Mongolia, Pakistan, Tajikistan, Turkmenistan, Uzbekistan, and Xinjiang Uyghur Autonomous Region.

[33]   Statistical, Economic and Social Research and Training Centre for Islamic Countries (SESRIC). 2018. *Strategic Roadmap for Development of Islamic Tourism in OIC Member Countries*. Ankara. Hajj and Umrah are Islamic pilgrimages. Hajj is one of the five pillars of Islam. It is obligatory for every Muslim once in their lifetime, provided they are physically fit and financially capable. Hajj is performed over specific days during a designated Islamic month. Umrah, however, can be performed at any time. Although they share common rites, Umrah can be performed in less than a few hours while Hajj is more time-consuming and involves more rituals.

[34]   UNWTO. 2020. *World Tourism Barometer*. 18(1). Madrid.

[35]   New intermediation businesses refer to travel and tourism digital global platforms (e.g., Airbnb, Booking, Expedia), airlines' tour operation programs (e.g., Ryanair, Easyjet, Wizzair), and several online travel agents.

of customers. Hence, to mitigate the impact of COVID-19 in this tourism segment, a label guaranteeing the hygiene of facilities could be developed and certified for the CAREC region, creating synergies and cross visitation among countries, and exploiting the image of uncrowded and exotic destinations. New waterside developments in Asia and Middle East are increasingly considered trendy and fashionable, but the boom in such destinations is related to connectivity and service quality. Therefore, the availability of flights at reasonable prices, as well as the presence of recognized accommodation brands that promote high service standards, should be considered as key prerequisites for success for destinations catering to this segment in the region.

29. **Health and wellness.** Health tourism represents 14.8% of the global wellness industry and it grew at a CAGR of 6.5% from 2015 to 2017.[36] The number of wellness tourism trips totaled 830 million in 2017, generating $639 billion worldwide ($770 per trip). Wellness customers look for differentiation and authenticity. Thus, destinations should develop products focused on their own wellness traditions and typical products to compete successfully. The CAREC region has the potential to promote itself as a destination rich in fresh air and open spaces, especially in those source countries where overpopulation and air pollution are major issues. Strict hygienic standards should be applied in accommodation and transport facilities to promote the CAREC region as a destination with a safe and healthy environment. This will be particularly important in the post-COVID-19 period. Exclusive services should be created, personnel should be trained, and facilities should be structured to develop a complementary offer for tourists coming to the region for other purposes such as business and adventure.

D. National Tourism Priorities and the Need for a Regional Tourism Strategy

30. All CAREC countries have developed national tourism strategies and plans to guide the development of their tourism sectors. The vision and objectives outlined in countries' national tourism strategies present common features such as increased focus on sustainability, preservation of natural and cultural resources, and improvement of international competitiveness and innovation within the tourism sector. Their main goals are to foster economic growth, generate jobs, and improve the quality of life of their citizens.

31. Most CAREC countries focus their respective national strategies on the following priorities: (i) sustainable development of tourism assets through responsible planning and management, and sound environmental and social protection; (ii) improved tourism institutional structures and governance; (iii) reduction of seasonality effects; (iv) improvement of air and land connectivity, and accessibility; (v) effective tourism branding and promotion in international markets; (vi) improvement of tourism and urban infrastructure, and tourism services and quality standards; (vii) digitalization of the sector; and (viii) attraction of private sector investments and development of public–private partnerships (PPPs). A summary of countries' national strategies is included in Appendix 1.

---

36   Global Wellness Summit. 2019. *Global Wellness Trends Report*. Miami.

32.   While individual CAREC countries possess outstanding resources for the development of their tourism sectors, each country's potential can be significantly increased through enhanced cooperation. Cooperation on visa and cross-border arrangements can facilitate travel between CAREC countries and enhance movement of people and goods across borders, bringing increased mutual benefits for each of the countries. Harmonization of tourism education and training systems and operating standards of tourism services can help produce the requisite number of qualified personnel and help address supply–demand gaps in the regional market. Joint market research, common statistical systems, and collaborative marketing activities can lead to better understanding of visitors' needs and greater customization of services, leading to increased tourism flows in the region.

33. Overall, regional tourism cooperation provides greater opportunities for economies of scale, reduced costs, and optimization of resources, and it can facilitate the development of competitive and resilient year-round destinations. Adopting such a regional approach to tourism revenue generation is particularly important given the adverse impacts of the COVID-19 pandemic on countries' tourism sectors and the substantial resources and investments that will be required as part of the recovery process.

CAREC Tourism Strategy 2030

A. Vision

34. The proposed vision for the CAREC region is to create *"a sustainable, safe, easily accessible, and well-known tourism region that provides a variety of unique year-round quality experiences to visitors along the Silk Road, and widely shares its benefits among its communities."*

B. Guiding Principles

35. The following guiding principles will underpin the development of comprehensive and effective regional tourism programs, and the promotion of tourism cooperation in the region:

(i) **Prioritizing quality over quantity.** Traditionally, countries' tourism strategies and actions have been oriented toward increasing the number of visitors to accelerate economic growth. However, a vast influx of tourists can severely burden countries, particularly those lacking the necessary infrastructure and capacities to effectively manage it. This can have a detrimental social and environmental impact and can result in a negative experience for visitors. Thus, careful consideration will be given to ensuring the right balance between the development of touristic assets in the CAREC region to attract visitors and the preservation of the social, cultural, and ecological values of the tourism areas to be developed. Improving the perceived quality of tourism services provision and increasing CAREC countries' capacity and awareness on the use and integration of sustainable practices in tourism programs and projects are key for this purpose.

(ii) **Adapting to global trends and building resilience.** The CAREC Tourism Strategy 2030 will be aligned with national tourism priorities and will help promote the uniqueness of each country's tourism products while focusing on building regional synergies and creating greater opportunities for economies of scale and optimization of resources to effectively respond and adapt to emerging global trends. Strengthening collaboration between countries to create safe travel corridors that enable a smooth and safe flow of tourists across the region and with distant markets, developing common health and safety tourism protocols and standards, building capacity of tourism stakeholders, increasing the private sector's participation and leadership roles in tourism development initiatives, and implementing joint tourism promotion initiatives are key elements to build resilience of countries' tourism sectors.

(iii) **Reducing regional imbalances and empowering local communities.** Many of the region's tourism assets are in rural areas of CAREC countries. The CAREC Tourism Strategy 2030 will contribute to bridging regional inequality gaps by fostering sustainable tourism growth in both urban and rural areas and providing opportunities for local communities to flourish. Gender equality through generation of jobs and income opportunities for private sector SMEs and entrepreneurs, including women and youth, will be promoted.

(iv) **Promoting multi-seasonal tourism through product diversification.** Based on its resources, the CAREC region can cater to diverse tourist segments and experiences, including adventure tourism, ecotourism, cultural tourism, architectural heritage tourism, religious tourism, recreational tourism, and business and city break tourism. Under the CAREC Tourism Strategy 2030, regional clusters that combine different tourism products and experiences across countries will be developed to help address seasonality and provide year-round opportunities for businesses in the region.

(v) **Adopting a holistic and phased approach for developing the CAREC tourism network.** The CAREC Tourism Strategy 2030 will seek to expand the network of tourism routes and strengthen the linkages between routes in a gradual manner to ensure sustainable and adequate growth of the regional tourism clusters. The development of safe travel corridors and tourism clusters will build upon existing routes such as the transnational historical Silk Road and other routes, such as the Pamir Highway, Karakorum Highway, Chinggis Khaan Trail, and Trans-Siberian Railway. Development of new cultural and religious routes will also be considered. Initiatives and projects to develop the tourism clusters will be prioritized based on countries' needs and priorities, with the aim of generating large regional benefits and attracting markets that will yield the highest returns. Given the cross-cutting nature of the tourism sector, careful consideration will be given to ensure close coordination across the wide range of stakeholders, including government agencies, the private sector, academia, and civil society.

C. CAREC Tourism Development Concept and Regional Tourism Priority Clusters

36. The proposed regional tourism concept under CAREC is based on the Silk Road as the most important tourism asset for the entire region and the basis for a common regional tourism umbrella brand. It aims at maximizing the international recognition of the Silk Road brand to further develop the various tourism market segments (paras. 18–29) through the development of regional tourism priority clusters. The following main routes and bypasses within the Silk Road are proposed (Figure 5):

(i) **Silk Road north route.** This route connects Urumqi, Almaty, Bishkek, Shymkent, Tashkent, Samarkand, Buchara, Merv, Ashgabat, Turkmenbashi, Baku, Tbilisi, and Batumi. Two bypasses are proposed for the north route: one through Issyk-Kul lake to Osh, Fergana, Khujand, and Samarkand; and another from Shymkent, Turkestan, Kyzlorda, Aral, Kulsary, Atyrau, and then by sea or air to Baku.

(ii) **Silk Road south route.** This route connects Hotan, Kashgar, Islamabad, Lahore, Hyderabad, Karachi, and Gwadar. The south route also has two bypasses: one from Kashgar, Sary-Tash, and Osh; and another from Islamabad, Peshawar, Kabul, Herat, and Merv.

37. In addition, two other important routes directly connected with the Silk Road have been taken into consideration: (i) a segment of the Trans-Siberian Railway, and (ii) the Chinggis Khaan Trail. The Trans-Siberian Railway connects north Mongolia with the Inner Mongolia Autonomous Region in the PRC, and the northeast part of the Inner Mongolia Autonomous Region with Beijing, which, although not being part of CAREC, is a major gateway to the region. The Chinggis Khaan Trail provides an adventure- and culture-driven experience from Delüün Boldog in Khentii *aimag* (provincial administrative unit in Mongolia), the place where Chinggis Khaan was born, to Ulaanbaatar (Mongolia) and west Kazakhstan.

38. Seven priority tourism clusters have been identified in the CAREC region based on regional relevance; visitation levels (in terms of domestic

visitors and foreign visitors from neighboring countries and distant markets); and the future development potential to attract an increasing number of tourists, increase spending per tourist, and improve the contribution of the tourism sector to countries' GDP.[37]

39. The routes mentioned in paras. 36–37 comprise the major national and transnational roads in the region, linking CAREC countries' major cities and tourism assets within the priority clusters (Appendix 2 lists the provinces and cities under each priority cluster group). Each priority cluster has at least one air hub in a major city with the potential to serve the overall cluster and connect the tourism assets within the cluster through various multimodal transport options. The seven priority clusters are as follows:

(i) **Caspian.** This cluster covers four countries (Azerbaijan, Georgia, Kazakhstan, and Turkmenistan) linked by air and sea. This cluster is oriented toward the adventure, city, business, culture, and sun and beach tourism segments.

(ii) **Heart of Central Asia.** This cluster covers six countries: Afghanistan, Kazakhstan, the Kyrgyz Republic, Tajikistan, Turkmenistan, and Uzbekistan. It focuses on the tourism segments of culture, adventure, city, and business.

(iii) **Almaty–Bishkek.** This cluster refers to the economic corridor between Almaty and Bishkek and the area around the Tian Shan mountains, including Issyk-Kul lake, Alaqol, Illi, and Aksu. It covers three countries (Kazakhstan, the Kyrgyz Republic, and north Xinjiang Uyghur Autonomous Region in the PRC) and it caters to the business, city, culture, adventure, and sun and beach tourism segments.

(iv) **Golden Coast.** This cluster, located in the southwest of Pakistan, is a coastal area spanning about 700 kilometers from Karachi to the Iranian border along the coast of the Arabian Sea. It has great potential for the sun and beach, adventure, culture, and business tourism segments.

(v) **Karakorum–Wakhan.** This cluster covers the eastern part of Afghanistan, southeast Tajikistan, north Pakistan, and northwest Xinjiang Uyghur Autonomous Region. This cluster focuses on the adventure, business, city, and culture segments.

(vi) **Altai.** This cluster spans the area from Urumqi to the Altai region, covering three countries: Mongolia, Kazakhstan, and the PRC. It is suitable for the adventure, ecotourism, business, and culture segments.

(vii) **Gobi and Grasslands.** This cluster forms a triangle extending from Delüün Boldog, Bayan-Ovoo to Ulaanbaatar (Mongolia) to Hohhot (Inner Mongolia Autonomous Region in the PRC). The main tourism segments are business, city, culture, and adventure.

---

[37] A cluster consists of an organized stock of touristic assets in a short-spatial distance that combine a series of touristic activities lasting at least 1 day. A mapping exercise of 1,447 tourism assets in the region was performed during March–June 2020. These assets were initially grouped into 49 small-scale clusters and scored in terms of visitation levels, regional relevance (priority was given to clusters covering more than one country and/or single-country clusters with important spillover effects on other CAREC countries either through an improved image of the region, potential of the core market segments addressed by the cluster, and/or potential to generate tourism flows to other CAREC countries), and the clusters' future development potential. Based on the scoring, the 49 small-scale clusters were further grouped into seven larger regional tourism priority clusters.

Figure 5: CAREC Tourism Development Concept and Clusters

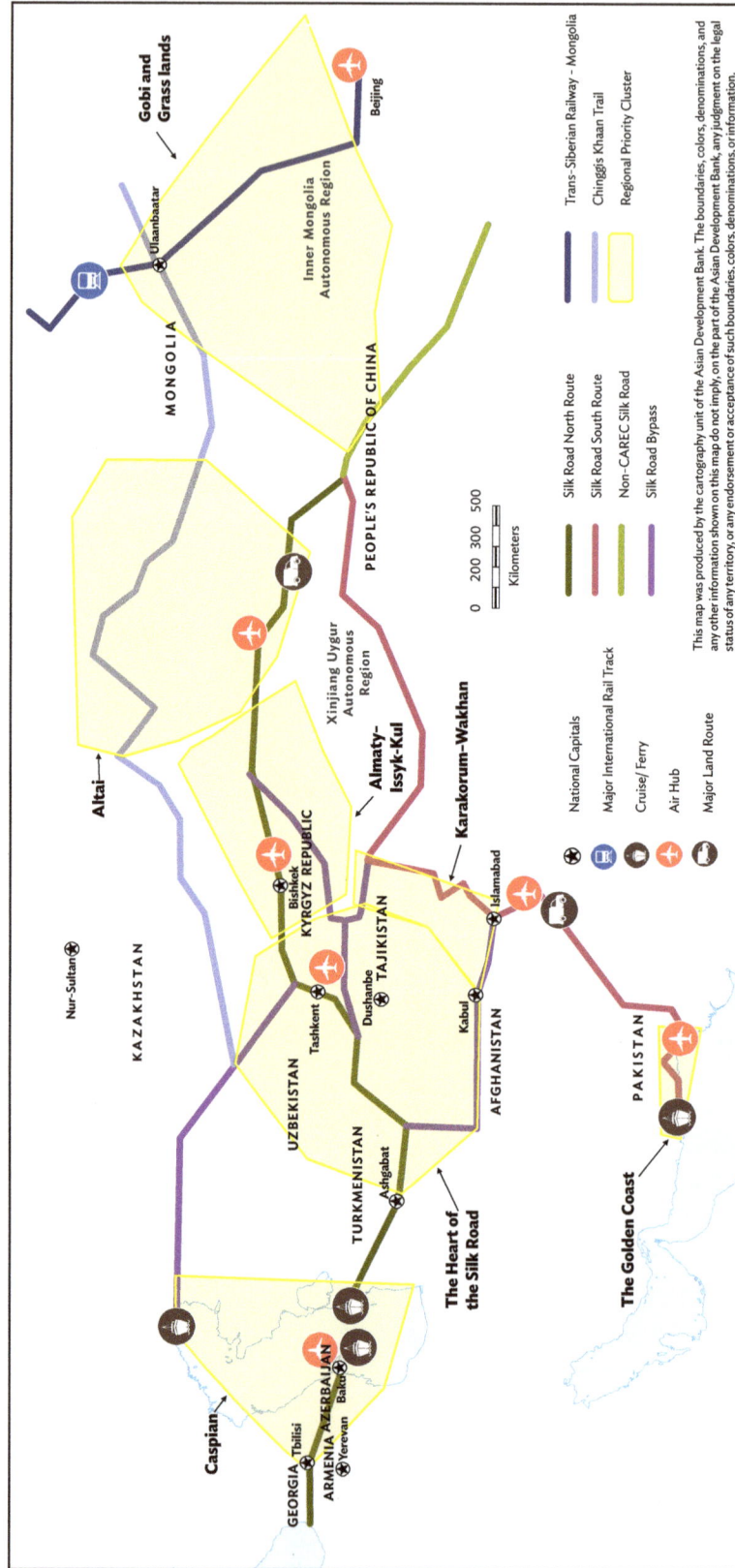

CAREC = Central Asia Regional Economic Cooperation.

Strategic Pillars of the CAREC Tourism Strategy 2030

40. The strengths of CAREC countries as tourism destinations arise from their wide range of unspoiled natural assets; historic cities and United Nations Educational, Scientific and Cultural Organization (UNESCO) World Heritage Sites; diverse ethnic groups and cultures; quality of lodging in capital cities; and strong government support for tourism development. Of particular importance is the countries' low population density, which allows the promotion of the region as a safe tourism destination and acceleration of post-COVID-19 recovery for each country's tourism sector. In spite of the slowdown in tourism because of the COVID-19 pandemic, the growing interest of travelers in new experiences and off-the-beaten track destinations, and the use of information technology to access tourism-related information and purchase tourism products and experiences, will continue playing a key role once international travel resumes. CAREC countries can take advantage of these trends while further exploiting the international recognition of the Silk Road by expanding the range of itineraries based on this well-known historical route.

41. Several factors, however, represent a significant barrier to the development of the tourism sector in the region. Access to and between CAREC countries is a fundamental requirement for national and regional tourism to grow. Transport facilities need to be improved to internationally accepted standards, with services on a regular and reliable basis. Border control arrangements and visa requirements should be tourist-friendly and more uniform across countries to facilitate intra-regional tourism and multicountry trips. This is not the case in all CAREC countries. Inconsistent quality of tourism infrastructure and services, skills shortages, and a challenging business environment are also key factors hindering tourism development in the region. Furthermore, market knowledge of CAREC countries is generally low (though growing in some instances) and necessitates promotional actions to create awareness of and interest in the tourist attractions of the countries on a regional basis.

42. To achieve the long-term tourism vision (para. 34), it is necessary to develop a strategic framework that builds on the region's main tourism strengths, addresses its main weaknesses, captures the main opportunities, and is resilient to the main threats. The strengths, weaknesses, opportunities, and threats analysis is summarized in Table 2.

43. Based on the strengths, weaknesses, opportunities, and threats analysis, the CAREC Tourism Strategy 2030 identifies five key strategic pillars with regional scope and where the implementation of regional initiatives and projects can help countries reap the socioeconomic benefits of sustainable tourism development (Figure 6). These pillars are (i) connectivity and infrastructure, (ii) quality and standards, (iii) skills development, (iv) marketing and branding, and (v) market intelligence. Cross-cutting themes will be mainstreamed in all interventions under the five strategic pillars, including safety and security,

Table 2: Strengths, Weaknesses, Opportunities, and Threats Analysis

Strengths	Weaknesses
• Outstanding unspoiled natural assets, and unique tangible and intangible cultural heritage and diversity in all CAREC countries • Low population density, even in capital cities, making it a safe tourism destination • Diversity and uniqueness of nomadic and settled cultures across the entire region, as well as ethnic groups and religions • Historic cities, legacy from ancient empires, and UNESCO World Heritage Sites in all countries • Quality of lodging and other tourism facilities in capital cities • Unknown destination suitable for discovery • Internationally recognized common brand: Silk Road • Local populations highly receptive to welcome tourists • Political goodwill and support from governments for tourism development	• High cost and poor air connectivity between CAREC capital cities and with distant markets • Inadequate transport infrastructure, roadside facilities on tourist routes, last-mile access, tourism services, and signage in tourist sites • Cumbersome and time-consuming border crossing and visa procedures (including in airports) • Lack of brand awareness and image resulting in little knowledge of CAREC countries and a weak perception of them as tourism destinations • Limited capacity on social responsibility practices and preservation of tourism assets • Limited multi-seasonal product development and tourism experiences to appeal to the most attractive market segments • Language barriers and shortages of skilled workers, destination managers, and tourism guides
Opportunities	**Threats**
• Growing international interest in and exposure of the Silk Road • Continued expansion of international tourism, particularly among the fast-growing Asian markets, and travelers' quest for new experiences and off-the-beaten track destinations • Major regional infrastructure projects under development in the region • Continuing rise of information technology enabling prospective travelers to gather information and interact digitally with potential service providers • Tourism as an industry capable of supporting post-pandemic economic recovery • Donor support for bankable tourism projects	• Growing international health risks and geopolitical conflicts, with high potential impacts in the travel and tourism industry • Climate change with global warming and environmental degradation • Safety and security issues and political instability in some CAREC countries • Economic downturns in primary tourist-generating markets • Natural and human-created disasters

CAREC = Central Asia Regional Economic Cooperation; UNESCO = United Nations Educational, Scientific and Cultural Organization.
Source: Consultant team under Asian Development Bank. 2019. *Technical Assistance for Sustainable Tourism Development in the Central Asia Regional Economic Cooperation Region*. Manila.

digital technology, gender, environmental sustainability, private sector participation, and universal access to tourism services. In addition, appropriate institutional and governance arrangements need to be in place to ensure effective implementation, monitoring, and evaluation of the CAREC Tourism Strategy 2030.

Figure 6: CAREC Tourism Strategic Pillars

Institutions and Governance

| Connectivity and Infrastructure | Quality and Standards | Skills Development | Marketing and Branding | Market Intelligence |

Cross-Cutting Themes: Health, Safety, and Security; Digitalization; Gender; Environmental Sustainability; Private Sector Participation; Universal Access

CAREC = Central Asia Regional Economic Cooperation.
Source: Consultant team under Asian Development Bank. 2019. *Technical Assistance for Sustainable Tourism Development in the Central Asia Regional Economic Cooperation Region.* Manila.

A. Strategic Pillar 1: Connectivity and Infrastructure

44. **Key challenges.** Air connectivity is key for the development of the tourism sector in CAREC countries given the landlocked nature of the region. High transport costs, limited air connectivity, cumbersome border crossings, and poor road conditions represent major obstacles to the development of intra-regional and international tourism in the CAREC region. The development of the aviation sector in CAREC countries is constrained by high ground costs, limited competition and protectionist aviation policies, and ineffective regulatory frameworks. Difficulties in land connectivity arise from poor last-mile access conditions to tourism sites, and the need to upgrade road and rail infrastructure in terms of quality and the provision of roadside services. Although investments in upgraded rail connections in CAREC countries are taking place with support from international development partners, freight movement has been the priority. In addition, complex border crossing arrangements (e.g., visa requirements and cost, immigration and passport control systems, and time for clearance) act as a significant deterrent to the development of the tourism sector in the region. Furthermore, most tourism assets are focused on the spring and summer months in regions with good potential for year-round activities; these assets therefore require investments in capacity and quality to reduce their seasonality and improve private sector profitability in tourism businesses.

45. **Proposed actions.** The CAREC Tourism Strategy 2030 will focus on making CAREC countries more accessible by facilitating border crossing procedures, easing visa requirements, and improving air connectivity by reducing ground costs and harmonizing aviation regulatory frameworks. Regional initiatives and projects under this pillar will be implemented in close coordination with the work being

conducted under other CAREC operational clusters, such as transport and trade.[38] Proposed areas of intervention will include the following:

(i)   Improvement of air connectivity to and between CAREC countries, with development of affordable non-European Union-banned[39] air services into gateway airports and capital cities in the region.

(ii)   Liberalization of visa regimes and automation of entry requirements that are common across CAREC countries.

(iii)   Simplification of border crossing procedures for foreign tourists, improvement of technological means of processing people and vehicle crossings, and upgrade of infrastructure and immigration facilities.

(iv) Improvement of ferry crossings for passengers and vehicles between Caspian cities along the coast for the Caspian Sea as well as accessibility from the seaports to the nearest tourist centers.

(v)   Improvement of road and rail connectivity to reduce travel time between tourism clusters and key tourism assets in the region.

(vi)   Improvement of public transport and last-mile access, signage, information points, roadside services, and quality and availability of sanitary facilities and toilets[40] in key tourism attractions and rest areas along tourist routes.

(vii) Rehabilitation of existing tourism assets and development of new tourism infrastructure and facilities in areas with potential for year-round activities within the priority tourism clusters. These initiatives could be implemented through private sector investments or through PPP arrangements with means of de-risking the investments.[41]

(viii) Improvement of basic services such as water supply, sewage, and solid waste management in urban and rural areas around the most visited tourism assets of the priority tourism clusters.

(ix)   Development of a common registry of tourism assets to allow effective and cost-efficient use by public entities, government officials, travelers, guides, and tour operators.

B.   Strategic Pillar 2: Quality and Standards

46.   **Key challenges.** Tourism services in the CAREC region are mostly provided by SMEs, except for the presence of some large international hotel chains. SMEs do not have either the resources or the know-how to implement quality standards. Development and implementation of harmonized service quality and environmental standards aligned with international best practices, including those related to health and safety, are key to raising the competitiveness of the region as a global tourism destination, and attracting tourists from high-spending markets.

---

[38]   These will include priority investment projects included in the CAREC Transport Strategy 2030, and projects and activities included in ADB. 2019. *CAREC Integrated Trade Agenda 2030 and Rolling Strategic Action Plan, 2018–2020.* Manila.

[39]   The European Union has the strictest aviation regulations in the world, and being allowed to fly there represents a strong trustworthiness instrument for third countries in relation to reliability, safety, and security.

[40]   These could include eco-friendly solutions for toilets in remote areas specially tailored for cold weather.

[41]   Such means could be, for example, concessions with the exclusive right to exploit mineral water springs for human consumption in exchange for the investments in infrastructure for tourists.

47. **Proposed actions.** One of the main features of the CAREC Tourism Strategy 2030 is the establishment of the common "Visit Silk Road" brand, which requires member countries to work in a coordinated and collaborative manner to protect and foster its brand value. This can be achieved, among other actions, through the establishment of effective and harmonized minimum service quality standards. Regional projects and initiatives within this pillar could include the following:

(i) Development of common minimum quality, hygiene, and environmental standards of tourism facilities, attraction sites, hotels, restaurants, means of transport, airports, trains, and bus stations. This could include the implementation of a star system for accommodation, which allows tourists to have an intuitive understanding of the expected quality level prior to booking, as well as the development of a "Silk Road Quality Label" for other tourism services, to be adopted on a voluntary basis.

(ii) Development and implementation of a system for registration of tourism businesses, and effective regionally harmonized inspection mechanisms for tourism service providers to ensure standards compliance.

(iii) Development and implementation of a formal claim management system for tourists in relation to tourism service providers, rewarding the best performers through effective promotion and positive reviews, and penalizing the poor service providers.

(iv) Support to tourism businesses, particularly SMEs and women-owned enterprises, to increase their capacity in the implementation of quality standards and access to efficient promotional tools. The "Silk Road Quality Label" would also help support promotion and marketing of those tourism businesses providing high-quality standards.

C. Strategic Pillar 3: Skills Development

48. **Key challenges.** All CAREC countries suffer from important shortcomings with regard to tourism skills. Public sector officials need more specialized and up-to-date knowledge in the development of effective tourism policies and strategies as well as in destination management and digital marketing, standards, safety and hygiene-related regulations, and environmental and socioeconomic sustainability policies. The private sector also requires improved knowledge in the development, management, and marketing of tourism products, services, and experiences. There is also a need to improve tourism education and training systems to ensure the necessary quantity and quality of graduates that can meet both current and future skills demand in the region. Online tourism skills development is in its infancy in CAREC countries, but this mode of learning is increasingly recognized as a cost-efficient model to invest in reducing the skills gap in the tourism sector, where a regional collaborative approach has the potential to generate important impacts. The COVID-19 outbreak is accelerating the trend of remote work and distance learning, giving further impetus to develop online learning solutions for the region.

49. **Proposed actions.** The CAREC Tourism Strategy 2030 will support CAREC member countries in addressing skills gaps by developing integrated tourism skills and training offerings through regional programs, and maximizing the use of digital technologies. Initiatives under this pillar will be developed and implemented in close coordination with the private sector to help close the gaps between industry practices and tourism education and training provision. Regional projects and initiatives within this pillar could include the following:

(i) Development of distance learning tourism programs to allow remote educational experiences for students and teachers, private sector representatives, and public officials, with certification issued by internationally accredited institutions and organizations, allowing for international skills recognition and acceptance.

(ii) Development of common curricula and qualifications for technical and vocational education and training and higher education levels to create an effective equivalence system for students who choose the technical and vocational education and training path and later choose to proceed with further studies. A related initiative could be the acceptance of diplomas and professional certificates of tourism professionals from across CAREC countries.

(iii) Improvement of the quality of tourism education and skills development programs in CAREC countries in alignment with international standards and best practices. This could be operationalized by setting up a joint tourism program in the region certified by the UNWTO through the TedQual Certification.[42]

(iv) Development of a platform that supports twinning programs between tourism education and training institutions within the region, and knowledge sharing across CAREC countries. Tourism education and training institutions in the region,[43] as well as the CAREC Institute, will be used for the provision of demand-driven capacity-building activities for tourism professionals on best practices in the development and management of tourism destinations.

(v) Promotion of intra-regional student mobility, including work and internship placements, and faculty exchanges.

(vi) Improvement of tourism professionals' skills through specialized training programs that are internationally accredited by reputable institutions and organizations with recognition in all CAREC countries. These could include tour guides (World Federation of Tourist Guide Associations), ski instructors (International Ski Instructors Association), travel agents (International Air Transport Association), and specialized training programs for MICE tourism, among others.

D. Strategic Pillar 4: Marketing and Branding

50. **Key challenges.** The Silk Road is the most important tourism asset shared by CAREC countries. Given its international recognition, it provides the ideal branding for the CAREC region's tourism. One of the most fundamental needs for CAREC countries is building a perception that the countries are, both individually and in combination, destinations that (i) offer a wide range of outstanding tourism experiences with high-quality facilities and standards; (ii) are easy to reach, travel around in, and travel between; and (iii) provide a safe and secure environment. This necessitates investments in marketing and promotion targeted at the most promising tourism segments, and oriented toward building back confidence in tourism destinations during the post-COVID-19 recovery period. However, CAREC countries face the challenge of budgetary restrictions for tourism marketing, promotion, and branding activities, which are key for effectively positioning the region globally.

[42] The TedQual Certification is a quality certification for tourism education and training programs offered by the UNWTO. The certification pays particular attention to ensuring that tourism education and training programs incorporate tourism industry and student employability needs. UNWTO. *TedQual Certification System.* https://www.unwto.org/unwto-tedqual-certification-system.
[43] This could include, for example, the Silk Road International University of Tourism in Samarkand.

51. **Proposed actions.** Investing in joint tourism promotion activities and sharing related costs will benefit all countries in the region. The CAREC Tourism Strategy 2030 will support regional tourism marketing and promotion initiatives focused on a common brand, including the following:

(i)   Creation and promotion of a common umbrella brand ("Visit Silk Road") through the development and management of a CAREC tourism web portal. The portal will serve as a regional tool for sharing and consolidating tourism-related information, and generating business opportunities for the private sector in CAREC countries by allowing the booking of package tours and experiences through the portal itself or through links to the websites of private sector-owned tourism businesses.

(ii)   Design of marketing strategies and promotional activities on a regional and/or cluster basis aimed at reinforcing the countries' image as safe tourism destinations to visit, restoring travelers' confidence, and reactivating tourism investments and demand in the region. As domestic and regional tourism is likely to return first in the post-COVID-19 recovery period, marketing and promotion activities will focus on neighboring countries in the short term, followed by international markets once travel restrictions are lifted further.

(iii)   Development of partnerships with major digital tourism platforms to run year-round campaigns for the entire region in selected target markets, in coordination with off-line promotional initiatives in these markets.

(iv)   Organization of and/or participation in tourism events with high promotional effects regionally and internationally (e.g., joint exhibitions and events to promote the tangible and intangible cultural diversity and uniqueness of the region, a Silk Road rally) that could contribute to the brand-building process.[44] Special attention will be given to initiatives that support business-to-business networking and information sharing for tour operators and other tourism services business providers.

(v)   Promotion of affordable multicountry travel on the Silk Road through common initiatives such as a "Silk Road Pass." The Silk Road Pass could include special fares for air and/or land transport within the CAREC region, visas, and discount coupons for other accredited tourism attractions and service providers in CAREC countries.

E.   Strategic Pillar 5: Market Intelligence

52. **Key challenges.** Tourism intelligence and knowledge are essential in developing targeted and innovative tourism products and services. Improving the gathering and analysis of tourism data and statistics and knowledge of customers' behavior is paramount in enhancing the international competitiveness of the CAREC region. Most CAREC countries do not have effective systems of data collection, statistics production, and collection of primary data to evaluate the performance of their products in relation to current and future customers' expectations. These shortcomings are a central problem that can be minimized with regional

---

44   Silk Road rally could be organized as a similar concept of the Dakar rally, but covering several CAREC countries.

cooperation. For example, the Tourism Satellite Accounts (TSA) is an international best practice and a key instrument to measure and monitor the impact of tourism policies and strategies in national economies.[45]

53.   **Proposed actions.** To address the existing challenges and shortcomings faced by most CAREC countries in terms of the availability and quality of data, market intelligence, and the production of statistics, the CAREC Tourism Strategy 2030 will focus on the following:

(i)   Support for the development and implementation of common methodologies for data gathering and production of tourism statistics, such as the International Recommendations for Tourism Statistics 2008 (footnote 14), to allow the public and private sectors to make evidence-based decisions.

(ii)   Development of methodologies and capacity strengthening of countries to conduct surveys on customers' satisfaction and spending patterns per tourist segment.

(iii)   Development and implementation of TSAs to measure and monitor the impact of tourism policies and strategies in the national economies.

(iv)   Support for the establishment of UNWTO observatories in CAREC countries to monitor the environmental and social impact of tourism at the destination level.[46]

(v)   Utilization of regional data collection and statistics production tools powered by effective digital solutions to allow cost-sharing across countries and the achievement of economies of scale.

(vi)   Promotion of partnerships between public and private tourism stakeholders in the region for conducting joint research and analyses focused on customers' behavior, preferences, desired experiences, and needs.

F.   Cross-Cutting Themes

54.   Several themes cut across all five strategic pillars, requiring that each of the regional programs and initiatives is shaped with the necessary considerations of such themes. These include the following:

(i)   **Health, safety, and security.** To support countries' efforts to respond to the COVID-19 pandemic and build resilience of their tourism sectors to future global crises, careful consideration will be given to the development and implementation of safety assurances and effective controls and health protocols, including through capacity building and information- and data-sharing mechanisms to avoid the spread of infectious diseases. The development of a pilot safe travel corridor and/or travel bubble in the short term will be paramount for rapid replicability across clusters.

---

[45]   The TSA is the main tool for the economic measurement of tourism. It allows for the harmonization and reconciliation of tourism statistics from an economic (national accounts) perspective. This enables the generation of tourism economic data (such as Tourism Direct GDP) that is comparable with other economic statistics. United Nations, Department of Economic and Social Affairs, Statistics Division; UNWTO; Eurostat; and Organisation for Economic Co-operation and Development. 2010. *Tourism Satellite Account: Recommended Methodological Framework 2008*. New York, Madrid, Luxembourg, and Paris.

[46]   The International Network of Sustainable Tourism Observatories was created in 2004 by the UNWTO to provide a framework for systematic, timely, and regular monitoring of resource use; the implementation of sustainable development plans and policies; and the impact of tourism at the destination level. In the CAREC region, there is only one observatory (Kanas observatory in Xinjiang Uyghur Autonomous Region), which focuses its efforts especially on monitoring tourism impacts in remote and border areas (the Kanas lake nature reserve in the Altai mountains borders Kazakhstan, Mongolia, and the Russian Federation).

(ii) **Digitalization.** Digital and communication technologies are at the center of the most lucrative activities of the tourism value chain. The CAREC Tourism Strategy 2030 will support the development and implementation of innovative solutions for the provision of tourism services, increased connectivity, improved destination marketing and promotion, and development of educational tools and digital tourism content.

(iii) **Gender equality.** Tourism policies, programs, and initiatives to ensure that both women and men have equal rights and equal access to resources, economic opportunities, education, training, and decision-making processes will be promoted.

(iv) **Private sector development.** Particular focus will be placed on increasing private sector participation and promoting private investments to implement regional programs and projects under the five strategic pillars. Support will be provided to strengthen tourism investment policies, laws, and regulations to create an enabling business environment and provide equal treatment for domestic and international investors, while fostering the development and implementation of innovative solutions in the sector.

(v) **Environmental sustainability.** Adoption of appropriate safeguard measures and sustainability practices to protect the region's natural tourism assets will be considered when developing and implementing regional tourism programs and projects.

(vi) **Universal access.** People with disabilities need to have access to tourist attractions and recreation facilities as well as tourism-related economic opportunities.[47] Special needs of the increasing proportion of elderly travelers will also need to be incorporated into destination planning and management, and marketing and promotion initiatives.[48]

---

[47] The senior tourism market segment may not be that familiar with online tools, so it is important that online marketing initiatives are combined with traditional communication channels.

[48] ADB. Forthcoming. *Georgia—Inclusive Cities: Urban Area Guidelines*. Manila.

Institutionalization and Implementation Arrangements

A. Phased Implementation Approach

55. To support the implementation of the CAREC Tourism Strategy 2030, a regional tourism investment framework, 2021–2025 has been developed, covering regional projects and initiatives under each of the five strategic pillars (Appendix 3). In alignment with the overall directions of the CAREC 2030 strategy (footnote 1), and in recognition of the varying levels of development and capacity of CAREC countries, flexibility will be built into the investment framework by allowing two or more countries to implement regional projects and initiatives agreed on by all member countries. The regional tourism investment framework will serve as a tool for prioritizing the projects and will allow for greater coordination among development partners and mobilization of resources. The CAREC tourism focal points group will be responsible for monitoring the implementation of the regional tourism investment framework on an annual basis and proposing adjustments as needed based on countries' emerging needs and priorities. A phased approach is suggested for the implementation of the proposed strategy for developing tourism in the region (paras. 56–58).

56. **Phase 1: Readiness improvement (2021–2023).** The COVID-19 outbreak is shifting travelers' priorities to closer and safer destinations in the short term. Thus, focusing on the development of domestic and intra-regional tourism will be key during this phase, while building up the foundations to attract high-spending tourists from international markets in the medium to long term. Initiatives during this phase will focus on skills development, including through the use of technology; adoption and implementation of common quality standards for tourism services, including health and safety protocols; improvement of data collection, statistics, and market intelligence; and development of the common "Visit Silk Road" brand, including through the development of the CAREC tourism web portal (para. 51).

57. **Phase 2: Rapid market share growth (2024–2028).** During this phase, the main aim will be increasing market share in lucrative international markets by improving connectivity, infrastructure, and regulatory procedures in the priority tourism clusters. Initiatives during this phase could include, among others, improvement of the aviation sector and air connectivity at low fares;[49] development of hubs with stopover features in the priority clusters; improvement of last-mile access and border crossing point

---

[49] This could include the development of a regional airline owned by various countries, following the Scandinavian Airlines (better known as SAS) model.

procedures within the priority cluster groups; harmonization of visa regimes and introduction of e-visas in all countries; improvement of ferry crossings of the Caspian Sea for passengers and cargo; feasibility assessment and establishment of a tourism investment fund with regional scope to support the private sector, PPP development, and public investment; and strong product development with emphasis on digitalization of supply and product offerings, e.g., the Silk Road Pass (para. 51).

58. **Phase 3: Consolidation of competitive positioning and improvement of value added (2029-onward).** In phase 3, the main target should be to strengthen the development programs of phases 1 and 2 within the priority cluster groups, and consider expanding toward the development of secondary destinations (beyond the priority clusters), provided that there is the necessary demand and ownership from member countries. Initiatives during this phase could include, among others, tourism promotion targeting specific areas within the priority clusters; further improvement of infrastructure and accessibility; and development of new tourism products to further diversify the offer of the different clusters.

B. Institutional Structure

59. The overall CAREC institutional framework will be taken as a starting point for setting up the appropriate institutional arrangements for tourism in the CAREC region (Figure 7). At the top, the CAREC Ministerial Conference functions as the main high-level policy and decision-

making body, responsible for providing strategic guidance on issues of regional relevance and accountable for the overall results of the CAREC Program. The Senior Officials' Meeting monitors progress on all operational clusters and sectors, recommends operational improvements, and ensures that the high-level decisions made at the CAREC Ministerial Conference are effectively implemented.

60. At the sector level, the overall CAREC tourism work will be led by a tourism focal points group. This group is composed of the tourism focal points appointed by each CAREC country since 2018.[50] The CAREC Secretariat will provide technical, administrative, and organizational support during the implementation of the CAREC Tourism Strategy 2030.

61. The CAREC 2030 strategy (footnote 1) advocates adopting an incremental approach in new operational areas such as tourism to effectively build countries' ownership and devise the most appropriate institutional structure based on progress made. The following four phases are proposed for the institutionalization of the CAREC tourism sector:

(i) **Phase 1.** Technical expert groups with both public and private sector representatives will be formed to further develop and coordinate the implementation of regional projects and initiatives within the strategic pillars.[51] Such technical expert groups will be focused and demand-driven to effectively support countries' emerging priorities and most pressing needs. During phase 1, only one or two technical expert groups will be constituted either at the thematic level (based on the themes

50 The tourism focal points were appointed by all CAREC countries in 2018 to support the formulation of the scoping study on Promoting Regional Tourism Cooperation under CAREC 2030 (footnote 2). Since then, two meetings of the tourism focal points group have been held (in October 2018 and December 2019).
51 Technical expert groups will include both national and provincial tourism stakeholders given the decentralization of the tourism sector in some CAREC countries (e.g., Pakistan).

Figure 7: CAREC Institutional Framework

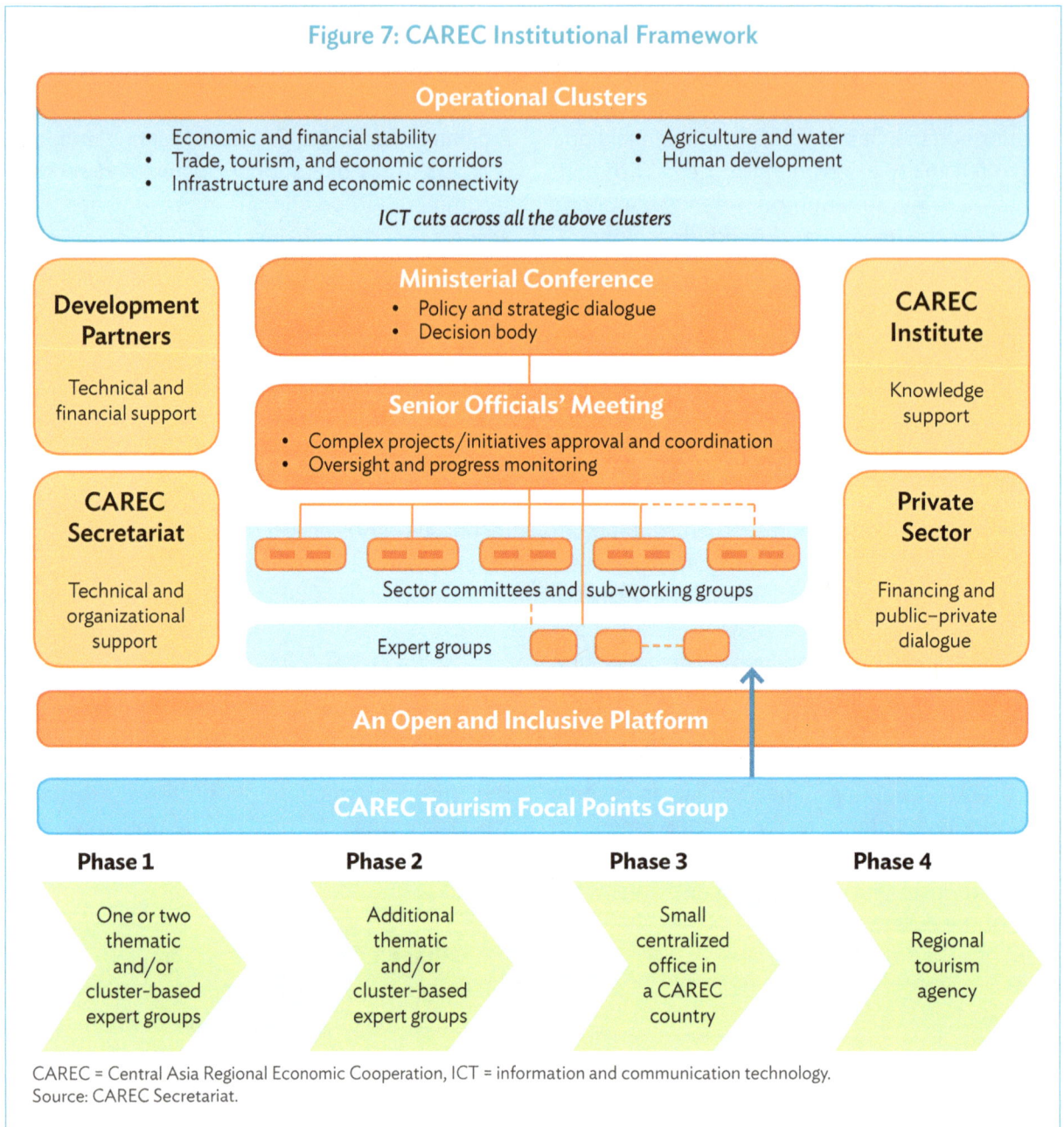

Operational Clusters

- Economic and financial stability
- Trade, tourism, and economic corridors
- Infrastructure and economic connectivity
- Agriculture and water
- Human development

ICT cuts across all the above clusters

Development Partners

Technical and financial support

Ministerial Conference
- Policy and strategic dialogue
- Decision body

CAREC Institute

Knowledge support

Senior Officials' Meeting
- Complex projects/initiatives approval and coordination
- Oversight and progress monitoring

CAREC Secretariat

Technical and organizational support

Sector committees and sub-working groups

Expert groups

Private Sector

Financing and public–private dialogue

An Open and Inclusive Platform

CAREC Tourism Focal Points Group

Phase 1 → One or two thematic and/or cluster-based expert groups

Phase 2 → Additional thematic and/or cluster-based expert groups

Phase 3 → Small centralized office in a CAREC country

Phase 4 → Regional tourism agency

CAREC = Central Asia Regional Economic Cooperation, ICT = information and communication technology.
Source: CAREC Secretariat.

and/or subthemes within the strategic pillars) and/or at the tourism cluster level should there be interest and demand from the countries that are part of such cluster.

(ii) **Phase 2.** When progress is considered sufficient and based on countries' demand, additional expert groups in other themes and/or subthemes and/or tourism clusters could be introduced. The additional expert groups would

work on the same manner as those referred to in phase 1. The tourism focal points group will continue overseeing the work of the focused expert groups and coordinating the overall work in the tourism sector.

(iii) **Phase 3.** When progress is considered sufficient by member countries and participating development partners in one or more themes of the strategic pillars and/or tourism clusters, a small office could be set up in a CAREC country to function as a centralized organizational unit to coordinate such thematic and/or cluster work.

(iv) **Phase 4.** A more permanent arrangement could be established in the form of an independent regional tourism agency. Depending on the progress achieved and the willingness of countries to deepen their cooperation, common funding mechanisms could be designed, and member countries could share the institutionalization costs. CAREC, as a neutral body, could support the establishment of this independent regional tourism agency, including supporting the appointment process of its executive board.

C. Financing

62. Financial resources are necessary to implement regional initiatives and projects, as well as national ones that can contribute positively to the overall development of tourism in the region. Financing is also needed to support the work of the tourism focal points group and the expert groups. Efforts will be devoted to mobilizing greater financing from a wide range of sources, including from development partners, state budgets, the private sector, and PPP arrangements. The Asian Development Bank (ADB) will strive to maintain technical assistance financing for the tourism sector. To support investments with regional scope and impact, the establishment of a regional investment fund will be explored in subsequent phases (para. 57). Such an investment fund could involve equity and lending components at affordable rates to promote the role of SMEs and the private sector in the development of the regional tourism industry.

D. Partnerships

63. A coordinated approach among all CAREC countries and development partners is required to implement the CAREC Tourism Strategy 2030. There are several national tourism initiatives and projects being implemented by various development partners and institutions in individual CAREC countries.[52] Building synergies among such initiatives through regular exchange of information and developing a collaborative partnership framework to combine financial and technical capabilities is important for maximizing the benefits of regional collaboration. In addition, mechanisms for developing partnerships with private entities in key areas such as data collection and statistics, education and skills development, and marketing and promotion will be promoted. The CAREC Institute can also play an important role in providing knowledge and analytical support across the five strategic pillars, particularly in the area of tourism skills development.

---

[52] These include (i) tourism initiatives under the Almaty–Bishkek Economic Corridor and the trilateral economic corridor initiative among Kazakhstan, Uzbekistan, and Tajikistan; (ii) ongoing and planned ADB tourism projects in Georgia, Tajikistan, Uzbekistan, and Mongolia (including the Strategic Framework Agreement for Sustainable Tourism Development, 2020–2021 between the Government of Mongolia and ADB); and (iii) tourism projects from other development partners such as the UNWTO and the UNESCO, among others.

E. Results Framework

64.   A results framework (Appendix 4) has been developed to periodically monitor and evaluate the implementation progress of the CAREC Tourism Strategy 2030 and its accompanying regional tourism investment framework. The CAREC tourism results framework is aligned with the overall CAREC 2030 results framework (footnote 1) and seeks to contribute, to the extent possible, to achieving performance targets and indicators in countries' national tourism strategies. The results framework includes indicators that are specific, measurable, achievable, relevant, and time-bound to monitor the strategy implementation progress at the outcome (vision) and output (strategic pillars) levels. Recognizing the global, changing nature of the sector and the fact that progress may be different within the strategic pillars and/or tourism clusters, flexibility will be built into the results framework, and the necessary adaptations will be reflected in the regional tourism investment framework on an annual rolling basis. Progress reports will be prepared and discussed among the CAREC tourism focal points on an annual basis and will be presented to the Senior Officials' Meeting. Progress reports will be made available online on the CAREC website and the regional tourism web portal.

Appendix 1:

Summary of CAREC Countries' Tourism Strategies

Country	Main Document	Strategic Priorities	Goals
Afghanistan	Draft Tourism Policy of Afghanistan (2020)	• Sustainable development, increased tourism revenues, and employment growth • Improvement of tourism products based on market needs • Infrastructure development based on international standards	Not specified
Azerbaijan	Tourism Strategy 2023 and key projects 2019 Strategic Road Map for the Development of Tourism Industry in the Republic of Azerbaijan (2016)	• Sustainable and growth-oriented tourism strategy • High diversity and competitiveness • Well-balanced regional and private sector development	To be achieved by 2020: • Increased number of foreign tourist overnights in Baku to a minimum of 3.65 million • Increased average length of stay from 2 to 3 days • Increased foreign tourist arrivals to 0.9 million, and foreign daily visitors to 1.5 million • Gradually accommodate 265,000 additional budget tourists • Increased capacity utilization rate to about 65% (occupancy rate) in wellness facilities • Attract 180,000 tourists to touristic attractions
China, People's Republic of	National: Thirteenth Five-Year Tourism Development Plan, 2016–2020	National: • Preparing strategic plans for the optimization of resources and market opportunities • Promoting innovation and quality • Supporting a tourism system that works in harmony with nature • Promoting inclusive growth by enhancing the quality of life and the satisfaction of people • Reforming destination management, tour guide, and travel agency systems • Strengthening coordination and cooperation with provincial and local governments	

continued on next page

A1 Table *continued*

Country	Main Document	Strategic Priorities	Goals
	Thirteenth Five-Year Tourism Development Plan of Inner Mongolia Autonomous Region, 2016–2020	**Regional:** Inner Mongolia Autonomous Region: • Preserving natural resources for sustainable development • Promoting diversity of resources • Promoting the integrated development of tourism, agriculture, culture, sports, and industry, focusing on quality and efficiency • Coordinating strategic planning to encourage year-round activity and to jointly promote the development of tourism products and routes • Stimulating innovation by assigning a decisive role to the market in terms of allocation of resources • Improving the effectiveness of government services and enhancing the provision of financial services	Inner Mongolia Autonomous Region, to be achieved by 2020: • Receive more than 130 million domestic and foreign tourists, with an average annual growth of more than 12% • Total revenue of the tourism industry to exceed CNY530 billion, with average annual growth of 20% or higher • Tourism's contribution to the provincial GDP to reach 15%
	Thirteenth Five-Year Tourism Development Plan—Xinjiang Uyghur Autonomous Region, 2016–2020	**Xinjiang Uyghur Autonomous Region:** • Opening up toward foreign tourism by taking advantage of the Silk Road Economic Belt • Improving transport systems and visa facilitation • Attracting capital investments and developing human resources • Innovating and developing tourism products • Building up a tourism industry that enriches people and aims at poverty alleviation, employment generation, and entrepreneurship • Promoting the development of smart tourism and the modernization of the tourism industry • Promoting structural reforms in the tourism sector	Xinjiang Uyghur Autonomous Region, to be achieved by 2020: • Total number of tourists to reach 300 million • Total tourism consumption to reach CNY600 billion • The number of people employed in tourism to reach 2.5 million, including 1 million in rural tourism poverty alleviation, driving 300,000 poor people out of poverty
Georgia	Georgian Tourism Development Strategy 2025	• Building the image of the country as a modern and safe tourist destination and increasing awareness • Increasing international arrivals and overnight stays, average spending by tourists, and revenues from tourism • Increasing the satisfaction of tourists and their loyalty • Improving international cooperation with tourism organizations, tour operators, MICE organizers, and international airlines	Not specified

continued on next page

A1 Table *continued*

Country	Main Document	Strategic Priorities	Goals
Kazakhstan	The State Program for the Development of the Tourism Industry of the Republic of Kazakhstan, 2019–2025	• Development of tourism assets • Transport accessibility of tourist destinations and assets • Quality and accessibility of tourism products and services • Favorable tourism climate • Effective system for promoting the country's tourism potential in domestic and international markets • Effective management system of the tourism sector	To be achieved by 2025: • Share of tourism in Kazakhstan's GDP of at least 8% • 9 million inbound visitors and 8 million domestic tourists • 650,000 people employed in the tourism industry • 2.5 times increase in the volume of tourist services to T270 billion • 3 times increase in investment in fixed assets to T600 billion • 80th position in the ranking of the World Economic Forum Travel and Tourism Competitiveness Index
Kyrgyz Republic	Tourism Development Program of the Government of the Kyrgyz Republic, 2019–2023	• Marketing and promotion of the Kyrgyz Republic as a center of tourism in Central Asia • Tourism digitization • Tourism development in the regions of the country • Creation of favorable conditions for doing business in the tourism sector and to attract investments	• The tourism sector should contribute 7% to GDP by 2023
Mongolia	Sustainable Development Concept 2030 National Strategy on Tourism Development, 2015–2025	• Increasing regional competitiveness by improving tourism infrastructure • Positioning Mongolia as a tourism brand internationally • Conducting activities to improve the public's knowledge and awareness on travel and tourism • Amending the tourism law • Providing tourism service providers with tax incentives • Providing better accessibility such as new and more frequent air routes, offering e-visa at borders, and supporting cross-border tourism	• Increasing the number of tourists in a phased manner: 1.0 million inbound arrivals by 2020, 1.5 million by 2025, and 2.0 million by 2030 • Implementing five new projects and programs in partnership with the UNWTO and international development institutions by 2020 • Improving Mongolia's ranking in the World Economic Forum's Travel and Tourism Competitiveness Index to the 85th position by 2025
Pakistan	Pakistan National Tourism Strategy Vision, 2020–2030	• Increasing tourism economic growth • Delivering a world-class visitor experience • Positioning Pakistan as a globally recognized tourism destination brand • Promoting responsible tourism practices	To be achieved by 2028: • Direct contribution of travel and tourism should be 3.0% of total GDP • Total contribution of travel and tourism should be 7.4% of GDP • Jobs directly supported by travel and tourism to increase by 2.7%, while those indirectly supported to increase by 2.3% • Visitor exports to increase to PRs192.5 billion

continued on next page

A1 Table *continued*

Country	Main Document	Strategic Priorities	Goals
Tajikistan	Development Strategy of Tourism in the Republic of Tajikistan for the period until 2030	• Strengthening tourism institutional framework • Developing modern tourist infrastructure • Ensuring competitiveness of tourism products by improving the quality of service • Developing and promoting the national brand as well as sub-brands of tourist areas • Marketing of tourism products • Development, protection, and rational use of natural recreational resources, as well as historical and cultural heritage • Strengthening human resources for productive employment in the tourism industry • Complying with international standards and ensuring the safety of tourists • Creating and developing tourism clusters and providing innovation and investments for the development of the tourist industry	To be achieved by 2030: • 2.5 million tourists visiting the country • Tourism contributes 8% to GDP and 15% to exports • 10% share of capital in the tourism industry and 3% share of tourism in state budget revenue • Services valued at $1,223.6 million provided in the tourism industry • 500 registered entities providing services in the field of recreation • Tourism industry accounts for 10% of total employment • 50th position in the ranking of the World Economic Forum Travel and Tourism Competitiveness Index
Turkmenistan	National Programme of Support and Development of Tourism in Turkmenistan for 2011–2020	• Establishment and development of a modern tourism system • Extensive tourism promotion in the country and abroad • Attraction of foreign investments • Development of tourism according to the strategies of environmental protection and reduction of seasonality	• In 2025, over 114,000 international travelers will visit the country • Digitalization of paperwork in the hotel sector, including electronic registration of travelers • Registration of hotels of Turkmenistan on international marketing platforms such as Booking.com, makemytrip.com, TripAdvisor., Trivago.ru • Training and retraining of personnel of the tourism sector per international standards and best practices in cooperation with the CAREC Institute • The attraction of investments for improvement of infrastructure around historical monuments
Uzbekistan	Decree of the President of the Republic of Uzbekistan on Additional Measures to Encourage Tourism Development in the Republic of Uzbekistan (2019)	• Improving the regulatory framework in tourism • Developing tourism infrastructure • Enhancing domestic routes and regional routes with neighboring countries • Adopting measures to reduce the influence of seasonal factors • Developing domestic tourism • Enhancing tourism promotion in domestic and foreign tourism markets • Improving the system of training highly qualified specialists, and advanced training of tourism service workers	To be achieved by 2025: • 11,810,000 foreign tourists visiting Uzbekistan • $2,170 million exports of tourist services • 25,010,000 domestic tourism trips • 3,050 hotels and similar accommodation facilities • 64,000 rooms in accommodation facilities • 128,000 beds in accommodation facilities • 1,450 tour operators

CAREC = Central Asia Regional Economic Cooperation; GDP = gross domestic product; MICE = meetings, incentives, conferences, and exhibitions; UNWTO = United Nations World Tourism Organization.

Sources: Consultant team under Asian Development Bank. 2019. *Technical Assistance for Sustainable Tourism Development in the Central Asia Regional Economic Cooperation Region*. Manila. Based on publicly available information and information provided by CAREC tourism focal points.

Appendix 2:

Indicative List of Provinces and Cities under Each Priority Tourism Cluster

Cluster	Country	Provinces and/or Regions	Main Cities
Caspian	Azerbaijan	Absheron, Aran, Daglig–Shirvan, Guba–Khachmaz, Lankaran	Astara, Baku, Ganja, Gobustan, Guba, Khachmaz, Lankaran, Mingachevir, Shabran, Sumgayit
	Georgia	Kakheti, Tbilisi	Gurjaani, Sagarejo, Tbilisi, Telavi
	Kazakhstan	Atyrau, Mangystau	Aktau, Atyrau, Kulsary, Zhanaozen
	Turkmenistan	Balkan	Balkanabat, Serdar, Turkmenbashi
The Heart of Central Asia	Afghanistan	Badakhshan, Badghis, Baghlan, Balkh, Bamyan, Faryab, Ghor, Herat, Jawzjan, Kabul, Kapisa, Kunduz, Laghman, Nuristan, Panjshir, Parwan, Sar–e Pul, Samangan, Takhar, Wardak	Bamyan, Chaghcharan, Charikar, Fayzabad, Herat, Kabul, Kunduz, Mahmud–I–Raqi, Maidan Shar, Maymana, Mazar i Sharif, Mihtarlam, Parun, Puli Khumri, Qala I Naw, Samangan, Sar–E Pol, Sheberghan, Taloqan
	Kazakhstan	Aktobe, Almaty, Atyrau, Jambyl, Kyzylorda, Mangystau, Turkistan	Aktobe, Almaty, Atyrau, Kyzylorda, Mangystau, Shymkent, Taraz, Turkistan
	Kyrgyz Republic	Batken, Jalal–Abadm, Osh	Batken, Jalal–Abad, Osh
	Tajikistan	Dushanbe, Khatlon, Kuhistani Badakhshan, Sughd	Dushanbe, Khorugh, Khujand, Kurganteppa
	Turkmenistan	Akhal, Lebap, Mary	Ashgabat, Mary, Turkmenabad
	Uzbekistan	Andijan, Bukhara, Djizzak, Ferghana, Karakalpakstan, Kashkadarya, Khorezm, Namangan, Navoi, Samarkand, Surkhandarya, Syrdarya, Tashkent	Andijan, Bukhara, Djizzak, Ferghana, Gulistan, Karshi, Namangan, Navoi, Nukus, Samarkand, Tashkent, Termez, Urgench
The Golden Coast	Pakistan	Balochistan, Sindh	Gwadar, Jiwani, Karachi, Ormara

continued on next page

A2 Table *continued*

Cluster	Country	Provinces and/or Regions	Main Cities
Karakorum–Wakhan	Afghanistan	Badakhshan, Kabul, Laghman, Kunar, Nangarhar, Nuristan	Jalalabad, Kabul
	Pakistan	Northern Pakistan, Khyber Pakhtunkhwa, Punjab	Gilgit, Islamabad, Mansehra, Peshawar
	People's Republic of China	Xinjiang Uyghur Autonomous Region	Kashgar, Tashkurgan
	Tajikistan	Kuhistani Badakhshan	Murghab, Rangkul, Shaymak
Almaty–Issyk-Kul	Kazakhstan	Almaty, Zhambyl	Almaty, Charyn, Chunja, Esik, Karabulak, Kaskelen, Kastek, Kegen, Kolsai, Korday, Masanchi, Samsi, Satti, Shelek, Talgar, Turgen, Uzynagach
	Kyrgyz Republic	Chuy, Issyk-Kul, Naryn	Bishkek, Cholpon-Ata, Karakol, Naryn
	People's Republic of China	Xinjiang Uyghur Autonomous Region	Aksu, Illi
Altai	Kazakhstan	East Kazakhstan	Ayagoz, Üst Kamenogorsk, Zaysan
	Mongolia	Bayan Ulgii, Govi-Altai, Hovd, Uvs	Altai, Hovd, Ulaangom, Ulgii
	People's Republic of China	Xinjiang Uyghur Autonomous Region	Altay, Karamy, Urumqi
Gobi and Grasslands	Mongolia	Bayankhongor, Darhan, Dornogovi, Dundgovi, Govisümber, Khentii, Omnogovi, Selenge, Töv, Ulaanbaatar	Bayankhongor, Chinggis, Choir, Dalanzadgad, Darkhan, Mandalgovi, Sainshand, Sükhbaatar, Ulaanbataar, Zuunmod
	People's Republic of China	Inner Mongolia Autonomous Region	Baotou, Bayannur, Hami, Hohhot, Turpan, Ulanqab, Xilingol

Source: Consultant team under Asian Development Bank. 2019. *Technical Assistance for Sustainable Tourism Development in the Central Asia Regional Economic Cooperation Region*. Manila.

Appendix 3:
Regional Tourism Investment Framework (2021–2025)

Tables A3.1–A3.5 contain a list of projects and initiatives under each of the strategic pillars of the Central Asia Regional Economic Cooperation (CAREC) Tourism Strategy 2030. The list is based on (i) analytical work conducted during the preparation of the strategy, (ii) feedback received from CAREC countries during the consultation workshops conducted during August–September 2020, and (iii) other projects and/or initiatives included under the strategies and actions plans of other operational clusters under CAREC. The list of projects will be subject to a prioritization process based on a set of criteria, including projects' alignment with the strategic pillars and integration of cross-cutting themes as well as projects' regional scope by either involving more than one country or having positive impacts in the tourism cluster and/or in at least another CAREC country. The prioritization process will be conducted by the CAREC tourism focal points group with support from the CAREC Secretariat. The CAREC tourism focal points group will also be responsible for monitoring the implementation of the regional tourism investment framework on an annual basis; adjustments will be made as needed based on countries' emerging needs and priorities.

Table A3.1: Strategic Pillar 1—Connectivity and Infrastructure

Project/Activity	Description	Cluster/Countries	Status	Indicative Implementation Period
Improvement of air connectivity and air travel cost reduction to and between Central Asia Regional Economic Cooperation (CAREC) countries[a]	Analysis on opportunities and challenges for introducing low-cost carriers in the CAREC region, including regulatory environment needs	All countries	Proposed	2021–2023
	Capacity-building activities on best practices in airport management, and aviation regulations and policies, including open skies agreements	All countries	Proposed	2021–2023
	Development of an air hub in Tashkent to serve as a main gateway to the Heart of Central Asia priority cluster	Uzbekistan with possible links to Afghanistan, Kazakhstan, the Kyrgyz Republic, Tajikistan, and Turkmenistan	Proposed	2021–2025
Liberalization of visa regimes and automation of entry requirements that are common across CAREC countries	Study on feasibility, requirements, and implications of a common and/or multicountry Silk Road visa in the CAREC region	All countries	Proposed	2021–2022
	Implementation of pilot Silk Road visa and/or analogue in some countries and/or priority cluster groups	At least three countries	To be defined	2022–2023

continued on next page

continued on next page

Table A3.1 *continued*

Project/Activity	Description	Cluster/Countries	Status	Indicative Implementation Period
Improved and automated border crossing procedures	Improvement of Sust border crossing point at the Pakistan–People's Republic of China (PRC) border	Pakistan, PRC	Proposed[b]	2021–2022
	Development of a new border crossing point at the Abreshumis Gza–Ipek Yolu friendship border crossing point	Azerbaijan, Georgia	Proposed[c]	2021–2022
	Improvement of facilities in the key border crossing points of the Silk Road routes	Uzbekistan	Proposed	2022–2025
Improvement of ferry crossings between major Caspian cities for passengers and vehicles	Development of tourism road map for the Caspian littoral states	Azerbaijan, Kazakhstan, Turkmenistan	Proposed	2021–2023
	Pre-feasibility study of alternative models for the ferry services, including public–private partnership arrangements.	Azerbaijan, Kazakhstan, Turkmenistan	Proposed	2022–2023
Improvement of road and rail connectivity to reduce travel time between tourism clusters and key tourism assets in the region	Construction of Tajikistan–Afghanistan–Turkmenistan railway	Afghanistan, Tajikistan, Turkmenistan	Proposed[b]	2023–2025
	Bukhara Region Road Network Improvement Project: M-37 Samarkand–Bukhara–Osh	Kyrgyz Republic, Uzbekistan	Proposed[b]	2021–2024
	Reconstruction of M-39 Road (Almaty–Bishkek–Tashkent–Termez)	Kazakhstan, Kyrgyz Republic, Uzbekistan	Proposed[b]	2021–2022
	Improvement of road conditions from Caspian seaports to the main touristic areas	Azerbaijan, Kazakhstan, Turkmenistan	Proposed	2023–2025
Improvement of tourism infrastructure, and support services and facilities for year-round activities	Improvement of existing and/or development of new tourism infrastructure in Jizzakh region bordering Tajikistan and Kazakhstan, including the Aydar-Arnasay lakes area	Uzbekistan with possible links to Kazakhstan and Tajikistan	Proposed	2021–2025

continued on next page

Table A3.1 *continued*

Project/Activity	Description	Cluster/Countries	Status	Indicative Implementation Period
	Improvement of existing and/or development of new tourism infrastructure in the mountain zones of Beldersay–Chimgan–Nanai of Bostanlyk district in Tashkent region	Uzbekistan with possible links to Kazakhstan and the Kyrgyz Republic	Proposed	2021–2025
	Improvement of existing and/or development of new tourism facilities and infrastructure in the Koytendag mountain area that borders Afghanistan and Turkmenistan	Turkmenistan with possible links to Afghanistan and Uzbekistan	Proposed	2021–2025
	Improvement of sanitary facilities and toilets in key tourism attractions and rest areas along tourist routes	Mongolia	Proposed	2023–2025
	Construction of tourist centers along the Silk Road, particularly in strategic border locations (e.g., Panjakent area near Samarkand)	Tajikistan with possible links to Uzbekistan	Proposed	2023–2025
	Development of recreational areas near Kowata underground lake near Ashgabat	Turkmenistan	Proposed	2023–2025
Development of a CAREC tourism assets' inventory	Establishment of a common digital database containing information about all tourism assets in CAREC countries, which can be hosted in the CAREC tourism web portal.	All countries	Proposed	2021–2022

[a] These initiatives will be implemented in coordination with the aviation pillar under the CAREC Transport Strategy 2030.
[b] Proposed project under the CAREC Transport Strategy 2030.
[c] Proposed project under the Rolling Strategic Action Plan, 2019–2021 under the CAREC Integrated Trade Agenda 2030.
Sources: Consultant team under Asian Development Bank. 2019. *Technical Assistance for Sustainable Tourism Development in the Central Asia Regional Economic Cooperation Region.* Manila.
        Also based on virtual country consultations held on 27 August 2020; and on 9, 10, and 11 September 2020.

Table A3.2: Strategic Pillar 2—Quality and Standards

Project/Activity	Description	Cluster/Countries	Status	Indicative Implementation Period
Development and implementation of common minimum quality standards	Development of a "Silk Road Quality Label" for tourism services (pilot project for demonstration)	Azerbaijan, Georgia	Proposed	2022–2025
	Implementation of a star system in accommodation services	Azerbaijan, Pakistan	Proposed	2022–2024
	Development and implementation of common health and safety protocols under the Almaty–Bishkek Economic Corridor	Kazakhstan, Kyrgyz Republic	Proposed	2020–2021
Development of a registry of tourism businesses	Establishment of a system for the registration of tourism businesses; the registry could be connected to the Central Asia Regional Economic Cooperation tourism web portal	Pilot project in at least two countries	Proposed	2023–2024
Capacity building and knowledge sharing on quality standards	Capacity building for tourism businesses, particularly small and medium-sized enterprises and women-owned enterprises, on the implementation of quality standards and access to efficient promotional tools	Azerbaijan, Pakistan	Proposed	2022–2024

Sources: Consultant team under Asian Development Bank. 2019. *Technical Assistance for Sustainable Tourism Development in the Central Asia Regional Economic Cooperation Region.* Manila. Also based on virtual country consultations held on 27 August 2020; and on 9, 10, and 11 September 2020.

Table A3.3: Strategic Pillar 3—Skills Development

Project/Activity	Description	Cluster/Countries	Status	Indicative Implementation Period
Harmonization of tourism education and skills standards	Development of common curricula and qualifications for technical and vocational education and training and higher education levels to allow recognition of diplomas and professional certificates of tourism professionals across Central Asia Regional Economic Cooperation (CAREC) countries	Azerbaijan, Turkmenistan, Uzbekistan	Proposed	2022–2024
Capacity building and intra-regional knowledge exchange	Trainings and capacity building programs for tourism professionals (both public and private sector), teachers, and students on best practices in the development and management of tourism destinations	All countries	Proposed	2021–2022
	Development of twinning programs between tourism education and training institutions within the region	Azerbaijan, Uzbekistan	Proposed	2022–2023
	Capacity building for the public and private sectors on the implementation and monitoring of health and safety measures and procedures	Kazakhstan, Kyrgyz Republic	Proposed	2020–2021
	Improvement of local tour guides' skills to effectively meet the needs and expectations of visitors from neighboring countries and distant markets while preserving natural and cultural tourism assets	All countries	Proposed	2022–2023

continued on next page

Table A3.3 *continued*

Project/Activity	Description	Cluster/ Countries	Status	Indicative Implementation Period
Online training and skills development	Development of an online tourism skills development program for CAREC countries, including tailor-made courses to address new and emerging tourism skills; cooperation with the United Nations World Tourism Organization Academy could be established for technical support and certification purposes	Azerbaijan, Kyrgyz Republic, Uzbekistan	Proposed	2021–2023

Sources: Consultant team under Asian Development Bank. 2019. *Technical Assistance for Sustainable Tourism Development in the Central Asia Regional Economic Cooperation Region.* Manila. Also based on virtual country consultations held on 27 August 2020; and on 9, 10, and 11 September 2020.

Table A3.4: Strategic Pillar 4—Marketing and Branding

Project/Activity	Description	Cluster/ Countries	Status	Indicative Implementation Period
Building and promoting a common umbrella brand "Visit Silk Road"	Development and operationalization of the Central Asia Regional Economic Cooperation (CAREC) tourism web portal as a regional tool for sharing and consolidating of tourism–related information, and generating business opportunities for the private sector in CAREC countries	All countries	Ongoing	2020–2021
	Development of the "Visit Silk Road" brand guidelines and strategy (e.g., positioning, guiding principles, logos, stationery, communication guidelines)	All countries	Proposed	2021–2022
	Organization of and/or participation in tourism events (e.g., joint exhibitions and events to promote the tangible and intangible cultural diversity and uniqueness of the region, a Silk Road Rally), and support for business-to-business networking and information sharing	All countries	Proposed	2021–2023
	Development of partnerships with major digital tourism platforms to run year-round promotional campaigns for the entire region in selected target markets, in coordination with off–line promotional initiatives in such markets	All countries	Proposed	2022–2024
Promotion of multicountry travel	Development of a "Silk Road Pass" to provide a more affordable option for visitors to undertake affordable multicountry trips within the region[a]	Azerbaijan, Mongolia, Uzbekistan	Proposed	2022–2023

[a] This initiative will be implemented in coordination with the aviation pillar under the CAREC Transport Strategy 2030.

Sources: Consultant team under Asian Development Bank. 2019. *Technical Assistance for Sustainable Tourism Development in the Central Asia Regional Economic Cooperation Region.* Manila. Also based on virtual country consultations held on 27 August 2020; and on 9, 10, and 11 September 2020.

Table A3.5: Strategic Pillar 5—Market Intelligence

Project/Activity	Description	Cluster/ Countries	Status	Indicative Implementation Period
Data collection, use of statistics, and measuring impacts of the tourism sector	Development and implementation of common methodologies (e.g., International Recommendations for Tourism Statistics 2008) for data gathering and production of tourism statistics	All countries	Proposed	2021–2023
	Development and implementation of Tourism Satellite Accounts to measure and monitor the impact of tourism policies and strategies in the national economies	Azerbaijan, Tajikistan, Uzbekistan	Ongoing (Tajikistan) Proposed (Azerbaijan, Uzbekistan)	2020–2022
	Support for the establishment of United Nations World Tourism Organization observatories in Central Asia Regional Economic Cooperation countries to measure and monitor the environmental and social impacts of tourism at the destination level	Azerbaijan, Georgia, Mongolia	Proposed	2022–2024
Market research	Capacity building for tourism agencies on the development and implementation of regular surveys on customers' satisfaction and spending patterns per tourist segment	Pilot project in at least two countries	Proposed	2022–2023
	Development of partnerships between public and private tourism stakeholders within the region for conducting joint research and analyses focused on customers' behavior, preferences, desired experiences, and needs	Azerbaijan, Uzbekistan	Proposed	2021–2022

Sources: Consultant team under Asian Development Bank. 2019. *Technical Assistance for Sustainable Tourism Development in the Central Asia Regional Economic Cooperation Region*. Manila. Also based on virtual country consultations held on 27 August 2020; and on 9, 10, and 11 September 2020.

Appendix 4:
Results Framework

Vision	Outcome Indicators	Source
A sustainable, safe, easily accessible, and well-known tourism region, that provides a variety of unique year-round tourism experiences to visitors along the Silk Road, and widely shares its benefits among its communities	By 2030: • Increased tourism's direct contribution to GDP (baseline 2019: $26.7 billion) • International visitor arrivals in the CAREC region increased (baseline 2019: 41.43 million) • CAREC countries' Travel and Tourism Competitiveness Index increased (base 100 index in 2019: 3.66)[a]	WTTC UNWTO, national tourism statistics WEF Travel and Tourism Competitiveness Reports

Strategic Pillars	Outputs	Output Indicators	Source
Connectivity and infrastructure	Improved multimodal connectivity and efficiency in border crossing procedures	• WEF Global Competitiveness infrastructure sub-index increased (base 100 index in 2019: 2.90)[a] • Seats capacity in air connections between CAREC countries increased (baseline 2019: 1.76 million seats)[b] • Number of countries with e-visa systems increased (baseline 2019: 7)	WEF Cirium SRS Analyser CAREC countries
Quality and standards	Enhanced service quality and minimum common standards adopted	• Travel and Tourism Competitiveness Index for tourist service infrastructure increased (base 100 index in 2019: 3.66)[a] • Harmonized service standards, including safety and hygiene protocols, adopted in at least two CAREC countries (baseline 2019: 0)	WEF CAREC countries
Skills development	Improved quality of tourism education and skills development programs and increased skilled workforce in the tourism sector in the region	• Travel and Tourism Competitiveness Index for human resources and labor market increased (base 100 index in 2019: 4.59)[a] • Number of tourism professional certificates recognized in at least two CAREC countries increased (baseline 2019: 0) • Number of TedQual-certified programs with regional coverage increased (baseline 2019: 0)[c]	WEF CAREC countries CAREC countries, UNWTO
Marketing and branding	Improved image and positioning of the region as a global tourism destination	• Travel and Tourism Competitiveness Index for effectiveness of marketing and branding to attract tourists increased (baseline 2019: 4.37) • Increased number of visitors to the CAREC tourism web portal (baseline 2019: 0) • Number of joint tourism marketing and promotion initiatives involving at least two CAREC countries increased (baseline 2019: 0)	WEF CAREC tourism web portal CAREC countries

continued on next page

A4 Table *continued*

Strategic Pillars	Outputs	Output Indicators	Source
Market intelligence	• Strengthened and harmonized tourism data collection and analysis in CAREC countries	• Increased number of CAREC countries with Tourism Satellite Accounts (baseline 2019: 0)[d]	CAREC countries
		• Partnerships between public and private institutions for conducting joint tourism research and analyses increased (baseline 2019: 0)	CAREC countries
Cross-cutting Themes	• Improved digitalization, sustainability, and inclusiveness of the tourism industry in CAREC countries	• Travel and Tourism Competitiveness Index for information and communication technology readiness increased (base 100 index in 2019: 4.31)[a]	WEF
		• Travel and Tourism Competitiveness Index for safety and security increased (base 100 index in 2019: 5.38)[a]	WEF
		• Travel and Tourism Competitiveness Index for health and hygiene increased (base 100 index in 2019: 5.74)[a]	WEF
		• Travel and Tourism Competitiveness Index for environmental sustainability increased (base 100 index in 2019: 3.84)[a]	CAREC countries
		• Number of women employed in the tourism industry in CAREC countries increased (baseline: TBD)[e]	CAREC countries
Institutions and governance	• Institutional mechanism for implementing joint regional tourism initiatives in CAREC established	• Thematic and/or cluster–based technical expert groups between two or more CAREC countries established (baseline 2019: 0)	CAREC Secretariat

CAREC = Central Asia Regional Economic Cooperation, GDP = gross domestic product, TBD = to be determined, UNWTO = United Nations World Tourism Organization, WEF = World Economic Forum, WTTC = World Travel and Tourism Council.

[a] The base 100 index for the starting year (2019) results from the simple average of the score of each country.

[b] This figure refers to air connections between 10 CAREC countries, excluding the People's Republic of China (PRC). Seats capacity in air connections between the PRC (national level) and other CAREC countries was 1.73 million seats in 2019. Disaggregated data for Xinjiang Uyghur Autonomous Region and Inner Mongolia Autonomous Region not available.

[c] The TedQual Certification is a quality certification for tourism education and training programs offered by the UNWTO. The certification pays particular attention to ensuring that tourism education and training programs incorporate tourism industry and student employability needs. There are three institutions with TedQual-certified programs in CAREC countries. However, none of these programs has regional scope.

[d] None of the CAREC countries compile the 10 tables of the tourism satellite account as per United Nations, Department of Economic and Social Affairs, Statistics Division; UNWTO; Eurostat; and Organisation for Economic Co-operation and Development. 2010. *Tourism Satellite Account: Recommended Methodological Framework 2008*. New York, Madrid, Luxembourg, and Paris. Kazakhstan compiles tables 1–7.

[e] Data not available. Production of gender–disaggregated statistics will be part of the proposed initiatives on the improvement of tourism data and statistics. A baseline for this indicator will be determined in coordination with CAREC countries at a later stage as the implementation of the strategy progresses.

Sources: Consultant team under Asian Development Bank. 2019. *Technical Assistance for Sustainable Tourism Development in the Central Asia Regional Economic Cooperation Region*. Manila. Also based on virtual country consultations held on 27 August 2020; and on 9, 10, and 11 September 2020.